A Collection of Australian Bush Verse

First published in Australia in 1989 by:
Peter Antill-Rose and Associates Pty Ltd
8/10 Anella Avenue
Castle Hill
New South Wales 2154
Australia

Telephone (02) 899 2766
Facsimile (02) 899 2775

Copyright© Peter Antill-Rose and Associates Pty Ltd 1989

Photographs copyright© Gary Lewis 1989.
Photographs by Gary Lewis
Pictorial editing by Allan Cornwell

Designed by Small Back Room Productions, Upwey, Victoria
Typeset by Bandaid Productions, Fitzroy, Victoria
Printed by Owen King Printers, Mulgrave, Victoria

ISBN 1 86282 034 1

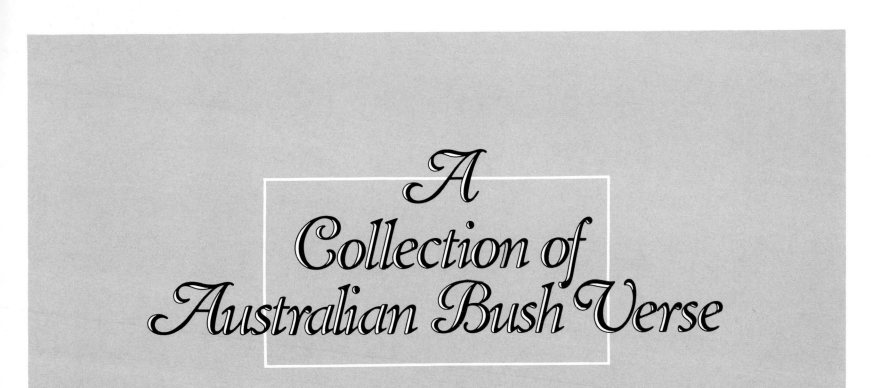

A Collection of Australian Bush Verse

Peter Antill-Rose
and Associates
Pty Ltd

8/10 Anella Avenue
Castle Hill New South Wales
2154 Australia

Contents

Introduction

'Banjo' Paterson deserves our gratitude not only for his wonderful poems, but also for rescuing from oblivion many of our old songs and ballads which, until his *Old Bush Songs* collection, had survived precariously. By 1910, only the old hands knew the songs, and the oral tradition was dying. Although we no longer learn these songs and ballads at our parent's knee, nonetheless the bush tradition is still strong, and many Australians know 'The Wild Colonial Boy', 'The Eumerella Shore', 'The Dying Stockman', or 'The Old Bark Hut', all first collected by Banjo Paterson when they were in danger of being forgotten. Most of these songs and ballads have a vigour and lively humour that belies the hardships of the early European settlers, and this readiness to mock and to 'knock', this dry sardonic humour, characterises many of the verses of Australia's later writers. Occasionally there is perhaps, especially in Henry Lawson's work, an excess of sentimentality, but there are also tender, moving verses acknowledging the loneliness, sorrow and despair of ordinary men and women facing a new and inhospitable land.

The lives of many of Australia's first white poets and balladists were sometimes as colourful and as tragic as the people they described.

Barcroft Boake was born in Sydney in 1866 of immigrant Irish parents, was adequately educated, then at 20 took to the bush, claiming that bush life was 'the only life worth living'. His own brooding nature is reflected in his emphasis on the tragedy and despair of bush life. *Where the Dead Men Lie*, his only book of poetry, was published five years after he hanged himself with his stockwhip at the age of 26.

Edward Dyson was born a year earlier than Barcroft Boake near the Victorian goldfields, where he spent his childhood. He worked first as a miner, then took up writing and journalism. Not surprisingly the two poems in this collection are set in mining areas. Best known for his short stories, his ballads are nonetheless remarkable for the insights they provide into the life of the underground miner.

Ernest Favenc, born in England in 1845, came to Australia when he was 19 and worked on stations in northern Queensland till he was 33. He then turned to exploring, opening up country along the south-west coast of the Gulf of Carpentaria and into Western Australia. These experiences of the lonely inland provided him with plenty of material for the many works of fiction and non-fiction he produced. His one volume of poetry, *Voices in the Desert*, was published in 1905, three years before his death.

William Montgomery Fleming, born in 1874 in the Wimmera, spent much of his long life as a parliamentarian, and most of his best literature was produced for children. He contributed both verse and prose to the *Sydney Morning Herald* and the *Bulletin*.

Adam Lindsay Gordon was born in the Azores in 1833, educated in England, and finally banished to South Australia in 1853 after his youthful exuberance got him into a number of scrapes. He worked briefly as a mounted policeman, then made a living riding and dealing in horses. In the years after his marriage, he settled by the sea near Mount Gambier, and most of the stories of his daring horsemanship come from that time, including his famous and hair-raising Blue Lake Leap. After a string of disasters he moved to Melbourne where he continued to write, but depression and melancholy overwhelmed him. In 1870, facing financial ruin, he shot himself on Brighton Beach, the day after his *Bush Ballads and Galloping Rhymes* was published. He is the only Australian poet to be honoured by a memorial in Poets' Corner in Westminster Abbey.

Charles Harpur was born in 1813 in Windsor, and raised in the Hawkesbury River district. During a long courtship he wrote many love sonnets to 'Rosa' (Mary Doyle) and finally married her in 1850. After some years as a farmer and public servant on the goldfields, a series of tragedies and misfortunes (including the death of his son in a shooting accident) marred his happiness. He had aspired to the position of 'Muse of Australia', attempting to produce Australia's first authentic poetic voice, but the lack of recognition during his lifetime made his final years bitter. He died in 1868, and much of his work was mangled by a meddling editor in a posthumous edition. Recent scholarship has restored his work and his reputation, which continues to grow.

Patrick Joseph Hartigan, alias John O'Brien, was born in Yass in 1878 and ordained as a Catholic priest in 1903. He administered the last rites to the man who was probably 'Banjo' Paterson's 'Man from Snowy River', and wrote poetry under his pseudonym, notably *Around the Boree Log*. 'Said Hanrahan' is one of his best poems.

Walter William Head was born in Oakleigh in Victoria in 1861. He was founding editor of the labour movement paper *Hummer*, later the *Worker*, and planned to go to Paraguay, but the death of his son prevented him. Henry Lawson's 'The Babies in the Bush' is based on the child's loss in the Victorian bush. After some financial difficulties he returned to editing and the labour movement in Tasmania. 'John Drayman' was the pseudonym he used when publishing his ballads.

Henry Kendall was born in 1839 on the south coast of New South Wales amidst the lush bush that inspired some of his best poems. His personal life was troubled and unhappy; alcoholism, the death of his daughter, marital problems and poverty undermined his writing. The Fagan family saw him through the blackest period and his rehabilitation. Reunited with his wife and family, he started work again, but his health failed and he died when only 43.

Henry Lawson, born on the New South Wales goldfields in 1867 to a Norwegian sailor and radical feminist publisher Louisa Lawson, was another writer who suffered from alcoholism. His early life was difficult, marked by poverty and parental discord, but by the age of 20 he had begun to publish his work in the *Bulletin*. Primarily a writer and editor, he also worked at odd jobs, including house painting on an influential trek to Bourke and Hungerford during a terrible drought. He married and continued to wander, as far afield as New Zealand and England. By the first decade of the new century Lawson's marriage had failed, his best work was behind him, and he was being treated in mental and convalescent hospitals for alcoholism between bouts of imprisonment. Friends continued to support him till his death, and his popularity was unaffected by his personal ruin. He was the first writer to be granted a State funeral.

Harry 'Breaker' Morant's origins are veiled in mystery. Born round 1864 in England, he came to Australia in 1883, working in a rodeo, and as a drover and horse breaker. He was briefly married to Daisy Bates in Charters Towers in 1884, and had a reputation as a wild and unpredictable man, but his skill as a horseman and poet, combined with a winning personality, earned him many friends. During the Boer War he ended up in the Bushveldt Carbineers, was tried for the murder of some Boer prisoners and a German missionary after his friend was killed and mutilated by Boers. Morant and another Australian were court-marshalled and shot, apparently sacrificed by Kitchener to appease the German government. His lively vigorous poems were published mostly in the *Bulletin* during his lifetime.

Will H. Ogilvie was born in Scotland in 1869 and came to Australia when he was 20, encouraged by his love of horses and adventure, and his admiration for Adam Lindsay Gordon. For 12 years he worked with horses in the outback and recorded his experiences in verses published in the *Bulletin* and other journals. His work is more romantic than many other Australian writers, and though he never returned to Australia, two volumes of his poetry were published in Sydney.

A. B. 'Banjo' Paterson was born on a station near Orange, New South Wales, in 1864. He grew up in the bush but moved to Sydney where he became a solicitor. Although his life was full of success, glamour and adventure, much of his work draws on his early experiences in the bush. He worked as a war correspondent during the Boer War, Boxer Rebellion and First World War, then worked as a journalist in Sydney with numerous stints in the country. Australia's greatest folk poet, Paterson still outsells any other volume of poetry with his *The Man from Snowy River*.

Thomas Edward Spencer, born in London in 1845, visited Australia when he was 18 and finally settled in Sydney in 1875. He worked as a building contractor and published various short stories, ballads, and a novel, but he is best known for his humorous ballads such as 'How McDougall Topped the Score'.

Jackeroos, Drovers and Stockriders

Jackeroos, Drovers and Stockriders

The most glamorous and highly esteemed job in the bush was that of the overlander. These drovers travelled with large numbers of sheep or cattle over vast distances in inland Australia, and like Saltbush Bill, they stole grass when they could from the despised squatters whose properties they crossed. Stockmen and jackeroos usually worked on stations, although given the immense size of some outback properties, their jobs, skills, and the risks they faced were often similar to those of the overlanders.

Drovers were natural riders, skilled in bushcraft, ready and able to use their stockwhips to good effect. Both horses and dogs were bred and trained to control stock and were highly valued, the dogs especially giving Australian drovers an edge over their American counterparts.

Cut off from the rest of the world like Paterson's Clancy, whose friends 'don't know where he are', these men had to rely on one another, hence perhaps the origin of the much-vaunted Australian mateship. But the hazards of the droving life were real enough: death by drowning, thirst, violence, or accident was not uncommon, and if the body survived these dangers, sometimes the mind did not. 'The Phantom Mob' is a sardonic account of one drover who lost everything, including his sanity.

Suffering and death were not confined to men of course, and Will Ogilvie, Henry Lawson, and W. M. Fleming are three poets who took the fate of stock, horses or dogs as the subject of some of their poems.

While the men were away with their cattle and sheep, the unsung women were managing small farms and facing the hazards of drought, flood, bushfire, isolation and childbirth. Perhaps it is not surprising that the men who wrote these poems and songs usually forgot to mention the women.

Occasionally sweethearts, wives, mothers, daughters or aunts appear in poems, but they are usually pining, waiting wistfully, or sometimes dying of grief — poets are a sentimental lot!

Andy's Gone With Cattle

Henry Lawson

Our Andy's gone with cattle now —
Our hearts are out of order —
With drought he's gone to battle now
Across the Queensland border.

He's left us in dejection now,
Our thoughts with him are roving;
It's dull on this selection now,
Since Andy went a-droving.

Who now shall wear the cheerful face
In times when things are slackest?
And who shall whistle round the place
When Fortune frowns her blackest?

Oh, who shall cheek the squatter now
When he comes round us snarling?
His tongue is growing hotter now
Since Andy crossed the Darling.

The gates are out of order now,
In storms, the 'riders' rattle;
For far across the border now
Our Andy's gone with cattle.

Poor Aunty's looking thin and white;
And Uncle's cross with worry;
And poor old Blucher howls all night
Since Andy left Macquarie.

Oh, may the showers in torrents fall,
And all the tanks run over;
And may the grass grow green and tall
In pathways of the drover;

And may good angels send the rain
On desert stretches sandy;
And when the summer comes again
God grant 'twill bring us Andy.

Andy's Return

Henry Lawson

With pannikins all rusty,
And billy burnt and black,
And clothes all torn and dusty,
That scarcely hide his back;
With sun-cracked saddle-leather,
And knotted greenhide rein,
And face burnt brown with weather,
Our Andy's home again!

His unkempt hair is faded
With sleeping in the wet,
He's looking old and jaded;
But he is hearty yet.
With eyes sunk in their sockets —
But merry as of yore;
With big cheques in his pockets,
Our Andy's home once more!

Old Uncle's bright and cheerful;
He wears a smiling face;
And Aunty's never tearful
Now Andy's round the place.

Old Blucher barks for gladness;
He broke his rusty chain,
And leapt in joyous madness
When Andy came again.

With tales of flood and famine,
On distant northern tracks,
And shady yarns — 'baal gammon!'
Of dealings with the blacks,
From where the skies hang lazy
On many a northern plain,
From regions dim and hazy
Our Andy's home again!

His toil is nearly over;
He'll soon enjoy his gains.
Not long he'll be a drover,
And cross the lonely plains.
We'll happy be for ever
When he'll no longer roam,
But by some deep, cool river
Will make us all a home.

11

Clancy of The Overflow

A.B. 'Banjo' Paterson

I had written him a letter which I had, for want of better
Knowledge, sent to where I met him down the Lachlan, years ago;
He was shearing when I knew him, so I sent the letter to him,
Just 'on spec', addressed as follows: 'Clancy, of The Overflow'.

And an answer came directed in a writing unexpected,
(And I think the same was written with a thumbnail dipped in tar);
'Twas his shearing mate who wrote it, and *verbatim* I will quote it:
'Clancy's gone to Queensland droving, and we don't know where
   he are.'

* * *

In my wild erratic fancy visions come to me of Clancy
Gone a-droving 'down the Cooper' where the Western drovers go;
As the stock are slowly stringing, Clancy rides behind them singing,
For the drover's life has pleasures that the townsfolk never know.

And the bush hath friends to meet him, and their kindly voices
   greet him
In the murmur of the breezes and the river on its bars,
And he sees the vision splendid of the sunlit plains extended,
And at night the wondrous glory of the everlasting stars.

* * *

I am sitting in my dingy little office, where a stingy
Ray of sunlight struggles feebly down between the houses tall,
And the foetid air and gritty of the dusty, dirty city
Through the open window floating, spreads its foulness over all.

And in place of lowing cattle, I can hear the fiendish rattle
Of the tramways and the buses making hurry down the street,
And the language uninviting of the gutter children fighting,
Comes fitfully and faintly through the ceaseless tramp of feet.

And the hurrying people daunt me, and their pallid faces haunt me
As they shoulder one another in their rush and nervous haste,
With their eager eyes and greedy, and their stunted forms
   and weedy,
For townsfolk have no time to grow, they have no time to waste.

And I somehow rather fancy that I'd like to change with Clancy,
Like to take a turn at droving where the seasons come and go,
While he faced the round eternal of the cashbook and the journal —
But I doubt he'd suit the office, Clancy, of the 'Overflow'.

The Cattle-dog's Death

Henry Lawson

The plains lay bare on the homeward route,
And the march was heavy on man and brute;
For the Spirit of Drought was on all the land,
And the white heat danced on the glowing sand.

The best of our cattle-dogs lagged at last,
His strength gave out ere the plains were passed,
And our hearts grew sad when he crept and laid
His languid limbs in the nearest shade.

He saved our lives in the years gone by,
When no one dreamed of the danger nigh,
And the treacherous blacks in the darkness crept,
On the silent camp where the drovers slept.

'The dog is dying', a stockman said,
As he knelt and lifted the shaggy head;
'Tis a long day's march ere the run be near,
And he's dying fast; shall we leave him here?'

But the 'super' cried, 'There's an answer there!'
As he raised a tuft of the dog's grey hair;
And, strangely vivid, each man descried
The old spear-mark on the shaggy hide.

We laid a 'bluey' and coat across
The camping pack of the lightest horse,
And raised the dog to his deathbed high,
And brought him far 'neath the burning sky.

At the kindly touch of the stockmen rude
His eyes grew human with gratitude;
And though we parched in the heat that fags,
We gave him the last of the water-bags.

The 'super's' daughter we knew would chide
If we left the dog in the desert wide;
So we brought him far o'er the burning sand
For a parting stroke of her small white hand.

But long ere the station was seen ahead,
His pain was o'er, for the dog was dead;
And the folks all knew by our looks of gloom
'Twas a comrade's corpse that we carried home.

A Thousand Mile Away

Hurrah for the old stock saddle, hurrah for the stock whip too,
Hurrah for the baldy pony, boys, to carry me westward ho;
To carry me westward ho, my boys, that's where the cattle stray,
On the far Barcoo where they eat nardoo, a thousand mile away.

Then give your horses rein, across the open plain;
We'll shift our meat both sound and sweet, nor care what some
   folks say;
And a-running we'll bring home them cattle that now roam
On the far Barcoo and the Flinders too, a thousand mile away.

Knee deep in grass we've got to pass, the truth I'm bound to tell,
Where in three weeks the cattle get as fat as they can swell;
As fat as they can swell, my boys, a thousand pound they weigh,
On the far Barcoo and the Flinders too, a thousand mile away.

No Yankee hide e'er grew outside such beef as we can freeze;
No Yankee pastures feed such steers as we send o'er the seas —
As we send o'er the seas, my boys, in shipments every day,
From the bar Barcoo where they eat nardoo, a thousand mile away.

So put me up with a snaffle, and a four or five inch spur,
And fourteen foot of greenhide whip to chop their flaming fur;
I'll yard them snuffy cattle in a way that I will swear,
Will make them Queensland cattlemen sit back in the saddle and
   stare.

Hurrah for the old stock saddle, hurrah for the stock whip too,
Hurrah for the baldy pony, boys, to carry me westward ho;
To carry me westward ho, my boys, that's where the cattle stray,
On the far Barcoo where they eat nardoo, a thousand mile away.

The Phantom Mob

W. M. Fleming, 'The Page'

Yes; I'm Harry Black — Mad Harry — and I often hear 'em say:
'Oh! he's off, poor chap; don't heed him — he has seen a better day.
He was king of all the drovers on a dry and dusty track;
He tried it once too often; it's Mad Harry — Harry Black.'

I had got a mob of cattle out beyond the back Paroo,
When stock-routes were the paddocks and fences far and few,
And the track was dry as wisdom, and the days were scorching hot,
The beasts were dropping off like flies — I thought we'd lose the lot.

And my mates were turning cranky — day and night without a
   drink —
But I kept 'em to the music, and I never slept a wink.
I *had* to keep 'em goin', or the beggars, beast and man,
Would have perished like a beetle in an empty billy-can.

I woke and found, one mornin' there was not a hoof alive!
But I rode around the bodies and started on to drive —
They were bloomin' hard to manage, but I kept 'em all the same,
For whoever knows Mad Harry will admit that he is game.

And I took 'em on my lonely, kept 'em movin' on the track,
Till the fellows who had left me one by one came sneakin' back.
And I never swore or cursed 'em — simply let 'em take a hand,
Till the curious way they watched me brought me round to
   understand.

I was drivin' ghosts o' cattle — not a live hoof in the lot! —
And they'd never camp a moment; though the day was blazin' hot,
And at night they never rested, always movin' movin' round,
With a restless sort o' movin' and a moanin' sort of sound.

Till at last I swore at Murphy, cursed Joe Cowly to his teeth,
And I saw their lips a-grinnin' and a skeleton beneath!
And I never swore or cursed 'em — simply let 'em take a hand,
They had travelled with the cattle, and were livin' men no more!

Ghosts o' men and ghosts o' cattle, I could see 'em through the day
In a strange and curious fashion and a hazy sort o' way;
And at night they gathered round me till my flesh was all a-creep,
And at last — I couldn't help it — while they watched I fell asleep.

Then they went and left me sleepin' — went and left me where I lay,
And I swore an oath I'd find 'em if I looked till Judgment Day!
Yes, I'm Harry Black — Mad Harry — and I never can forget
Those pikers from the back Paroo — I'm looking for 'em yet!

13

The Sick Stockrider

Adam Lindsay Gordon

Hold hard, Ned! Lift me down once more, and lay me in the shade.
Old man, you've had your work cut out to guide
Both horses, and to hold me in the saddle when I sway'd,
All through the hot, slow, sleepy, silent ride.

The dawn at 'Moorabinda' was a mist rack dull and dense,
The sunrise was a sullen, sluggish lamp;
I was dozing in the gateway at Arbuthnot's bound'ry fence,
I was dreaming on the Limestone cattle camp.
We crossed the creek at Carricksford, and sharply through the haze,
And suddenly the sun shot flaming forth;
To southward lay 'Katâwa', with the sandpeaks all ablaze,
And the flush'd fields of Glen Lomond lay to north.
Now westward winds the bridle path that leads to Lindisfarm,
And yonder looms the double-headed Bluff;
From the far side of the first hill, when the skies are clear and calm,
You can see Sylvester's woolshed fair enough.
Five miles we used to call it from our homestead to the place
Where the big tree spans the roadway like an arch;
'Twas here we ran the dingo down that gave us such a chase
Eight years ago — or was it nine? — last March.

'Twas merry in the glowing morn, among the gleaming grass,
To wander as we've wandered many a mile,
And blow the cool tobacco cloud, and watch the white wreaths pass,
Sitting loosely in the saddle all the while,

'Twas merry 'mid the blackwoods, when we spied the station roofs,
To wheel the wild scrub cattle at the yard,
With a running fire of stockwhips and a fiery run of hoofs;
Oh! the hardest day was never then too hard!

Aye! we had a glorious gallop after 'Starlight' and his gang,
When they bolted from Sylvester's on the flat;
How the sun-dried reed-beds crackled, how the flint-strewn
      ranges rang
To the strokes of 'Mountaineer' and 'Acrobat'.
Hard behind them in the timber, harder still across the heath,
Close beside them through the tea-tree scrub we dash'd;
And the golden-tinted fern leaves, how they rustled underneath!
And the honeysuckle osiers, how they crash'd!

We led the hunt thoughout, Ned, on the chestnut and the grey,
And the troopers were three hundred yards behind,
While we emptied our six-shooters on the bushrangers at bay,
In the creek with stunted box-tree for a blind!
There you grappled with the leader, man to man and horse to horse,
And you roll'd together when the chestnut rear'd;
He blazed away and missed you in that shallow water-course —

A narrow shave — his powder singed your beard!
In these hours when life is ebbing, how those days when life
      was young
Come back to us; how clearly I recall
Even the yarns Jack Hall invented, and the songs Jem Roper sung;
And where are now Jem Roper and Jack Hall?

Aye! nearly all our comrades of the old colonial school,
Our ancient boon companions, Ned, are gone;
Hard livers for the most part, somewhat reckless as a rule,
It seems that you and I are left alone.

There was Hughes, who got in trouble through that business with
      the cards,
It matters little what became of him;
But a steer ripp'd up MacPherson in the Cooraminta yards,
And Sullivan was drown'd at Sink-or-swim.

And Mostyn — poor Frank Mostyn — died at last a fearful wreck,
In 'the horrors', at the Upper Wandinong;
And Carisbrooke, the rider, at the Horsefall broke his neck,
Faith! the wonder was he saved his neck so long!
Ah! those days and nights we squander'd at the Logans' in the
      glen —
The Logans, man and wife, have long been dead.
Elsie's tallest girl seems taller than your little Elsie then;
And Ethel is a woman grown and wed.

I've had my share of pastime, and I've done my share of toil,
And life is short — the longest life a span;
I care not now to tarry for the corn or for the oil,
Or for the wine that maketh glad the heart of man.
For good undone and gifts misspent and resolutions vain,
'Tis somewhat late to trouble. This I know —
I should live the same life over, if I had to live again;
And the chances are I go where most men go.

The deep blue skies wax dusky, and the tall green trees grow dim,
The sward beneath me seems to heave and fall;
And sickly, smoky shadows through the sleepy sunlight swim,
And on the very sun's face weave their pall.
Let me slumber in the hollow where the wattle blossoms wave,
With never stone or rail to fence my bed;
Should the sturdy station children pull the bush flowers on
      my grave,
I may chance to hear them romping overhead.

Jim's Whip

Barcroft Boake

Yes, there it hangs upon the wall
And never gives a sound,
The hand that trimmed its greenhide fall
Is hidden underground,
There, in that patch of sally shade,
Beneath that grassy mound.

I never take it from the wall,
That whip belonged to *him*,
The man I singled from them all,
He was my husband, Jim;
I see him now, so straight and tall,
So long and lithe of limb.

That whip was with him night and day
When he was on the track;
I've often heard him laugh, and say
That when they heard its crack,
After the breaking of the drought,
The cattle all came back.

And all the time that Jim was here
A-working on the run
I'd hear that whip ring sharp and clear
Just about set of sun
To let me know that he was near
And that his work was done.

I was away that afternoon,
Penning the calves, when, bang!
I heard his whip, 'twas rather soon —
A thousand echoes rang
And died away among the hills,
As toward the hut I sprang.

I made the tea and waited, but,
Seized by a sudden whim,
I went and sat outside the hut
Watching the light grow dim —
I waited there till after dark,
But not a sign of Jim.

The evening air was damp with dew;
Just as the clock struck ten
His horse came riderless — I knew
What was the matter *then*.
Why should the Lord have singled out
My Jim from other men?

I took the horse and found him where
He lay beneath the sky
With blood all clotted on his hair;
I felt too dazed to cry —
I held him to me as I prayed
To God that I might die.

But sometimes now I seem to hear —
Just when the air grows chill —
A single whip-crack, sharp and clear,
Re-echo from the hill.
That's Jim, to let me know he's near
And thinking of me still.

The Flash Stockman

I'm a stockman to my trade and they call me 'Ugly Dave,'
I'm old and grey and only got one eye.
In a yard, I'm good, of course, but just put me on a horse
And I'll go where lots of young 'uns daren't try!

I'll lead them through the gidgee, over country rough and ridgy,
I'll lose them in the very worst of scrub.
I can ride both rough and easy, with a dewdrop, I'm a daisy!
And a right-down bobby-dazzler in a pub!

Just watch me use the whip, I can give the dawdlers gyp!
I can make the bloomin' echoes roar and ring.
With a branding-iron, well, I'm a perfect flamin' swell!
In fact, I'm dook of every blasted thing!

Just watch me skin a sheep, it's so lovely, you could weep,
I can act the silvertail as if my blood was blue!
You can strike me pink or dead, if I stood upon my head,
I'd be just as good as any other two!

I've a notion in my pate that it's luck, it isn't fate,
That I'm so far above the common run!
So, in everything I do, you could cut me fair in two!
For I'm much too bloody good to be in one!

15

Saltbush Bill

A. B. 'Banjo' Paterson

Now this is the law of the Overland that all in the West obey —
A man must cover with travelling sheep a six-mile stage a day;
But this is the law which the drovers make, right easily understood,
They travel their stage where the grass is bad, but they camp where
    the grass is good;
They camp, and they ravage the squatter's grass till never a blade
    remains,
Then they drift away as the white clouds drift on the edge of the
    saltbush plains;
From camp to camp and from run to run they battle it hand to hand
For a blade of grass and the right to pass on the track of the
    Overland.

For this is the law of the Great Stock Routes, 'tis written in white
    and black —
The man that goes with a travelling mob must keep to a half-mile
    track;
And the drovers keep to a half-mile track on the runs where the
    grass is dead,
But they spread their sheep on a well-grassed run till they go with a
    two-mile spread.
So the squatters hurry the drovers on from dawn till the fall of
    night,
And the squatters' dogs and the drovers' dogs get mixed in a deadly
    fight;
Yet the squatters' men, though they hunt the mob, are willing the
    peace to keep,
For the drovers learn how to use their hands when they go with the
    travelling sheep.

But this is the tale of a jackeroo that came from a foreign strand,
And the fight that he fought with Saltbush Bill, the King of the
    Overland.
Now Saltbush Bill was a drover tough, as ever the country knew,
He had fought his way on the Great Stock Routes from the sea to the
    big Barcoo;
He could tell when he came to a friendly run that gave him a chance
    to spread;
And he knew where the hungry owners were that hurried his sheep
    ahead;
He was drifting down in the 'Eighty drought with a mob that could
    scarcely creep —
When kangaroos by the thousand starve, it is rough on the travelling
    sheep.

And he camped one night at the crossing-place on the edge of the
    Wilga run,

'We must manage a feed for them here,' he said, 'or half of the mob
    are done!'
So he spread them out when they left the camp wherever they liked
    to go,
Till he grew aware of a jackeroo with a station-hand in tow,
And they set to work on the straggling sheep, and with many a
    stockwhip crack
They forced them in where the grass was dead in the space of the
    half-mile track;
And William prayed that the hand of Fate might suddenly strike him
    blue
But he'd get some grass for his starving sheep in the teeth of that
    jackeroo.

So he turned and he cursed the jackeroo, he cursed him alive or dead,
From the soles of his great unwieldy feet to the crown of his ugly
    head,
With an extra curse on the moke he rode and the cur at his heels
    that ran,
Till the jackeroo from his horse got down and went for the droving
    man;
With the station-hand for his picker-up, though the sheep ran loose
    the while,
They battled it out on the saltbush plain in the regular prize-ring
    style.
Now, the new-chum fought for his honour's sake and the pride of the
    English race,
But the drover fought for his daily bread with a smile on his
    bearded face —

So he shifted ground and he sparred for wind and he made it a
    lengthy mill,
And from time to time as his scouts came in they whispered to
    Saltbush Bill —
'We have spread the sheep with a two-mile spread, and the grass it is
    something grand,
You must stick to him, Bill, for another round for the pride of the
    Overland.'
The new-chum made it a rushing fight, though never a blow got
    home,
Till the sun rode high in the cloudless sky and glared on the brick-
    red loam,
Till the sheep drew in to the shelter-trees and settled them down to
    rest,
Then the drover said he would fight no more and gave his opponent
    best.

So the new-chum rode to the station straight, and he told them a
    story grand
Of the desperate fight that he fought that day with the King of the
    Overland.

And the tale went home to the Public Schools of the pluck of the
    English swell,
How the drover fought for his very life, but blood in the end must
    tell.
But the travelling sheep and the Wilga sheep were boxed on the Old
    Man Plain.
'Twas a full week's work ere they drafted out and hunted them off
    again;
With a week's good grass in their wretched hides, with a curse and a
    stock-whip crack,
They hunted them off on the road once more to starve on the half-
    mile track.

And Saltbush Bill on the Overland will many a time recite
How the best day's work that he ever did was the day that he lost
    the fight.

The Last Muster
Will H. Ogilvie

All day we had driven the starving sheep to the scrub where the axes
    ply,
And the weakest had lagged upon weary feet and dropped from the
    ranks to die;
And the crows flew up from the rotting heaps and the ewes too weak
    to stand,
And the fences flaunted red skins like flags, and the dour drought
    held the land.

And at night as I lay a-dreaming, I woke, and a silver moon
Shone fair on a dancing river and laughed to a broad lagoon,
And the grass turned over the fences and rippled like ripening grain,
And clouds hung low on the hilltops, and earth smelt sweet with the
    rain.

And in at the open window the lowing of cattle came —
A mob that had never a laggard and never a beast that was lame;
And wethers, a thousand thousand, and ewes with their lambs
    beside,
Moved over the green flats feeding, spread river to ranges wide.

And horses whinnied below me, and leaning I watched them pass,
Lusty and strong and playful like horses on spring-tide grass
When they whinny one to another, strong-voiced, and a gallop brings
Foam to the flank, be it only from paddock to stockyard wings.

Slowly they moved in the moon-mist, heads low in the cool
    night-dew,
Snatching the long bush grasses, breast-high as they wandered
    through;

Slowly they moved in the moon-mist, and never a horse on the plains
Was red with the gall of the collar or marked with a chafe of the
    chains.

And behind them a hundred drovers rode slow on their horses white,
All brave with their trappings of silver that flashed in the silver
    light;
Buckle and stirrup and bridle, and spurs for their better speed —
Singing behind the cattle like drovers on royal feed.

And I cooeed, and one came over that rode on the nearest wing,
And I called to him, 'Ho, there, drover! say, whose is the mob you
    bring?'
Then he reined his horse by the window, all silver-bitted and shod,
And spoke, and his words rang sadly, 'These are the cattle of God!'

So I said to him, 'Where are they bound for?' and he raised his hand
    to the West:
'They are bound for the star-fenced pastures on God's own rivers, to
    rest.'
And I asked him, 'Where did you muster?' and he answered me sadly
    again,
'From every gully and sandhill, from every valley and plain,

'From the swamps of the green kapunyah, from the reeds at the red
    creek-side,
From the thickets of twisted mulga, from the clay-pans furrowed and
    dried,
From the track to the Western goldfields, from the ruts of the Great
    North Road,
Where the dingoes go and the crows fly low we have gathered the
    beasts of God.'

And I said, 'Then has God repented because that He sent no rain?
And has God looked down in His pity on the poor dumb beasts He
    has slain?'
But the drover turned in his saddle and answered, his eyes in mine,
'Not so; for the beasts were slaughtered by man of his greed's design:
'God gave to them feed and water and pastures so wild and wide
They had fed him a thousand million from here to the ocean side;
But man in his greed came after and fenced them on hill and plain
And cursed the God in His heaven that would not send them His rain;

'And man's be the blame of the bleaching bone and the shame of the
    rotting hide,
And the pity of lorn lambs crying alone on the wind-swept mountain-
    side,
Of the weak horse down in his harness, of the bullock dead by the
    dray,
Of the moan of the thirsty cattle for ever and ever and aye!'

And he spoke to his steed and left me — moved out on the mist it seemed,
And I woke to the red burned acres, and knew that I had but dreamed.

The Drover's Sweetheart

Henry Lawson

An hour before the sun goes down
Behind the ragged boughs,
I go across the little run
And bring the dusty cows;
And once I used to sit and rest
Beneath the fading dome,
For there was one that I loved best
Who'd bring the cattle home.

Our yard is fixed with double bails,
Round one the grass is green,
The bush is growing through the rails,
The spike is rusted in;
And 'twas from there his freckled face
Would turn and smile at me —
He'd milk a dozen in the race
While I was milking three.

I milk eleven cows myself
Where once I milked but four;
I set the dishes on the shelf
And close the dairy door;
And when the glaring sunlight fails
And the fire shines through the cracks,
I climb the broken stockyard rails
And watch the bridle-tracks.

He kissed me twice and once again
And rode across the hill,
The pint-pots and hobble-chain
I hear them jingling still;
He'll come at night or not at all —
He left in dust and heat,
And when the soft, cool shadows fall
Is the best time to meet.

And he is coming back again,
He wrote to let me know,
The floods were in the Darling then —
It seems so long ago;
He'd come through miles of slush and mud,
And it was weary work,
The creeks were bankers, and the flood
Was forty miles round Bourke.

He said the floods had formed a block,
The plains could not be crossed,
And there was foot-rot in the flock
And hundreds had been lost;
The sheep were falling thick and fast
A hundred miles from town,
And when he reached the line at last
He trucked the remnant down.

And so he'll have to stand the cost;
His luck was always bad,
Instead of making more, he lost
The money that he had;
And how he'll manage, heaven knows
(My eyes are getting dim),
He says — he says — he don't — suppose
I'll want — to — marry — him.

As if I wouldn't take his hand
Without a golden glove —
Oh! Jack, you men won't understand
How much a girl can love.
I long to see his face once more —
Jack's dog! thank God, it's Jack! —
(I never thought I'd faint before)
He's coming — up — the track.

The Overlanders

There's a trade you all know well; it's bringing cattle over,
On every track to the Gulf and back, men know the Queensland
    drover!

So pass the billy round, boys, don't let the pint-pot stand there!
For tonight, we drink the health of every overlander!

I come from northern plains where the girls and grass are scanty;
Where the creeks run dry, or ten foot high, and there's grog in every
    shanty!

There are men from every land, from Spain, and France and
    Flanders,
They're a well-mixed pack, both white and black, the Queensland
    overlanders!

When we've earned a spree in town, we live like pigs in clover,
And the whole damn cheque pours down the neck of many a
    Queensland drover!

As I pass along the road, the children raise my dander,
Shouting, 'Mother dear, take in the clothes, here comes an
    overlander!'

A girl in Sydney Town, she says, 'Don't leave me lonely.'
I says, 'It's sad, but my old prad has room for one man only!'

Now I'm bound for home once more on a prad that's quite a goer;
I can find a job with a crawling mob on the banks of the Maranoa.

Ballad of the Drover

Henry Lawson

Across the stony ridges,
Across the rolling plain,
Young Harry Dale, the drover,
Comes riding home again.
And well his stock-horse bears him,
And light of heart is he,
And stoutly his old packhorse
Is trotting by his knee.

Up Queensland way with cattle
He's travelled regions vast,
And many months have vanished
Since home-folks saw him last.
He hums a song of someone
He hopes to marry soon;
And hobble-chains and camp-ware
Keep jingling to the tune.

Beyond the hazy dado
Against the lower skies
And yon blue line of ranges
The station homestead lies.
And thitherward the drover
Jogs through the lazy noon,
While hobble-chains and camp-ware
Are jingling to a tune.

An hour has filled the heavens
With storm-clouds inky black;
At times the lightning trickles
Around the drover's track;
But Harry pushes onward,
His horses' strength he tries,
In hope to reach the river
Before the floods shall rise.

The thunder, pealing o'er him,
Goes rumbling down the plain;
And sweet on thirsty pastures
Beats fast the plashing rain;
Then every creek and gully
Sends forth its tribute flood —
The river runs a banker,
All stained with yellow mud.

Now Harry speaks to Rover,
The best dog on the plains,
And to his hardy horses,
And strokes their shaggy manes:

'We've breasted bigger rivers
When floods were at their height,
Nor shall this gutter stop us
From getting home tonight!'

The thunder growls a warning,
The blue, forked lightnings gleam;
The drover turns his horses
To swim the fatal stream.
But, oh! the flood runs stronger
Than e'er it ran before;
The saddle-horse is failing,
And only half-way o'er!

When flashes next the lightning
The flood's grey breast is blank;
A cattle-dog and packhorse
Are struggling up the bank.
But in the lonely homestead
The girl shall wait in vain —
He'll never pass the stations
In charge of stock again.

The faithful dog a moment
Lies panting on the bank.
Then plunges through the current
To where his master sank.
And round and round in circles
He fights with failing strength,
Till, gripped by wilder waters,
He fails and sinks at length.

Across the flooded lowlands
And slopes of sodden loam
The packhorse struggles bravely
To take dumb tidings home;
And mud-stained, wet, and weary,
He goes by rock and tree,
With clanging chains and tinware
All sounding eerily.

The Death of Peter Clark

Hubert H. 'Barwon' Parry

The sun was blazing fiercely on the cracked and dusty plain
As Peter Clark the drover rode toward his home again.
For weeks he'd been a-droving, where the golden sunsets glow,
Behind the lowing cattle of a trail-herd moving slow.
With stockwhip ringing loudly as the breaking steer he wheeled
And curses shouted fiercely at the yapping dogs that heeled,
He'd taken cattle safely from his Lower Hunter home,
To where the Namoi River waters fields of reddened loam.

He rode with one companion, just a lad of fifteen years;
A gamer little stockman never cracked a whip at steers;
For when the herd was fractious or it broke in wild stampede
He'd ride to wheel the leaders and the danger never heed.
The lad could sit an outlaw, till the 'sky was underneath',
Whose eyes would roll and whiten as it bared the wicked teeth.
While saddle-girths were creaking with the sudden reefs and strains,
He'd sink the spur-rowels deeply as he loosed the foam-flecked reins.

The drovers rode in silence to the distant range of blue,
Where rise the giant Murrulla and the towering Tinagroo
In solitary grandeur, mighty monarchs of the range
That reign, their might unchallenged, o'er a kingdom wild and
    strange.
Like sentinels that guard the plains their rugged summits rise
Against the dim horizon, as in challenge to the skies;
And o'er the mighty gorges with a misty mantle hung
The soaring eagle circles o'er her unmolested young.

As on the drovers travelled through the lazy afternoon
The youngster's heart was happy and he gaily hummed a tune;
But Clark was grim and silent, as the horse he loved to ride
Moved on toward the ranges with a long and springy stride;
For early in the morning when they paused their mounts to change,
A squad of mounted troopers coming back from Warland's Range
Had said that dreaded Wilson, just a day or two before,
Had swooped and robbed the mail-coach of the golden freight it bore.

They warned the elder drover, but his laugh was cold and strange,
For well he knew, that evening, they must camp on Warland's
    Range.
As, winding up, the roadway passed where range and foothill met,
The drover knew they'd reach the spot just as the sun was set;
But loudly had he boasted that they'd camp on yonder hill:
No man in all the country could his heart with terror fill.
He'd camp in spite of Wilson, when the evening sun was low
And o'er the gloomy ranges cast its last departing glow.

The troopers had not argued, for they knew the drover well,
And knew he'd never waver at a devil straight from hell —

As tough and game a fighter as the country ever knew,
He'd fought on every stock-route from the coast to the Barcoo,
And never man could stop him when across the overland
He rode behind the cattle with that burnt and hardy band,
When drovers had to battle for the starving stock to pass
And squatters fought to keep them from the brown and dying grass.

They reached the camp as darkness cast her shadows o'er the
    ground
And soon the weary horses grazed contented close around.
The drovers by the fireside sat and drank their billy tea,
While round about the hobble-chains were clinking cheerily.
They talked of home and people, as the gentle evening breeze
Would waft the smoke in spirals through the branches of the trees,
Till, tired, they sought the solace of the peaceful land of sleep,
And never dreamed that danger through the silent night would
    creep.

But through the inky darkness came a sharp and stern command;
The drovers from their blankets were compelled to rise and stand —
Each man to face the shadow with his hands above his head;
One move, the man informed them, and he'd riddle them with lead.
But Clark was calm and silent, as the outlaw came in sight;
His thoughts were fast revolving, for he meant to rush and fight;
And as the dreaded Wilson sought the plucky drover's gold,
He sprang with arms extended seeking for a fatal hold.

A gunshot stabbed the darkness with a crimson jet of flame,
The wounded drover staggered, but he came on just the same,
And closed upon the outlaw with a grip of tempered steel;
His blood was flowing freely, but the wound he did not feel.
He strained and wrestled fiercely, as he fought to gain a holt
Upon the arm of Wilson and the hand that held the 'Colt'.
But in the deadly struggle, fate must play a leading part —
The gun, again exploding, shot the drover through the heart.

The drover fell, but falling, threw his powerful arms around
The body of the outlaw, as they crashed upon the ground;
And thus the plucky drover drew a last and fleeting breath,
With Wilson locked unconscious in the mighty grip of death.
The youngster, dumb with terror, as the two had fought and
    strained,
Had watched the battle, helpless, but his mind he now regained;
And rushing to his saddle for a length of green-hide rope
He bound the two together where they lay upon the slope.

Then, mounting quickly, galloped through the darkness of the night
To tell the mounted troopers of the drover's fatal fight.
With hoof-beats ringing loudly as the spur at every stride
Left blood from flank to shoulder on the sweating horse's side,
He brought the racing troopers, till the light of breaking day
Revealed the bloody camp-site, where in death the drover lay,
Wrapped sound in sleep eternal with his days of droving o'er,

Still tightly locked with Wilson, who would scourge the range no
   more.

And o'er the saddened country spread the tidings far and wide;
The mountain breezes mourning through the wattle blossom sighed;
But on the Lower Hunter, where the swaying willows sweep,
A someone's heart was bleeding for a drover wrapped in sleep.
Through Wingen, Scone and Blanford spread the story of the death,
And far away to westward, where the summer's scorching breath
The dying herbage withers, where the rolling plains are wide,
And horses groan and labour, as the teamster rides beside.

The Drover's Dream

One night when travelling sheep, my companions lay asleep,
There was not a star to 'luminate the sky;
I was dreaming I suppose, for my eyes were partly closed,
When a very strange procession passed me by.
First there came a kangaroo with a swag of blankets blue,
A dingo ran beside him as his mate;
They were travelling mighty fast, but they shouted as they passed,
'We'll have to jog along, it's getting late!'

The pelican and the crane they came in from the plain
To amuse the company with a highland fling;
The dear old bandicoot played the tune upon his flute,
And the native bears sat round them in a ring.
The drongo and the crow sang us songs of long ago;
The frill-necked lizard listened with a smile;
And the emu standing near with his claw up to his ear
Said: 'That's the funniest thing I've heard for quite a while!'

The frogs from out the swamp where the atmosphere is damp
Came bounding in and sat upon the stones.
They each unrolled their swags, and produced from little bags
The violin, the banjo, and the bones.
The goanna and the snake and the adder wide awake,
With an alligator danced 'The Soldier's Joy'.
In the spreading silky-oak the jackass cracked a joke,
And the magpie sang 'The Wild Colonial Boy'.

Some brolgas darted out from the tea-tree all about,
And performed a set of Lancers very well.
Then the parrot green and blue gave the orchestra its cue
To strike up 'The Old Log Cabin in the Dell'.
I was dreaming, I suppose, of these entertaining shows,
But it never crossed my mind I was asleep,
Till the boss beneath the cart woke me up with such a start
Yelling: 'Dreamy, where the hell are all the sheep?'

The Freehold on the Plain

I'm a broken-down old squatter, my cash it is all gone,
Of troubles and bad seasons I complain;
My cattle are all mortgaged, of horses I have none,
And I've lost that little freehold on the plain.

For the stockyard's broken down, and the woolshed's caving in;
I've written to the mortgagees in vain;
My wool it is all damaged, it is not worth a pin,
And I've lost that little freehold on the plain.

I started as a squatter some twenty years ago,
When fortune followed quickly in my train;
But I speculated heavy and I'd have you all to know
That I've lost that little freehold on the plain.

I built myself a mansion, and chose myself a wife;
Of her I have no reason to complain;
For I thought I had sufficient to last me all my life,
But I've lost that little freehold on the plain.

And now I am compelled to take up the drover's life,
Driving cattle through the sunshine and the rain,
And leave her there behind me, my own dear loving wife —
We were happy in that freehold on the plain.

The Stockman's Last Bed

Be ye stockmen or no, to my story give ear:
Poor Jack's gone aloft and no more shall we hear
The crack of his whip or his steed's lively trot,
His clear 'Go ahead!' or his jingling quart-pot.

We laid him where wattles their sweet fragrance shed
And the tall gum trees shadow the stockman's last bed.

While drafting one day he was horned by a cow.
'Alas!' cried poor Jack, 'it's all up with me now!
I ne'er shall be seen in the saddle again,
Or bound like a wallaby over the plain.'

His whip it is silent, his dogs they do mourn,
His horse looks in vain for its master's return.
No friends to bemoan him, unheeded he dies;
Save the wandering myall none cares where he lies.

Now, stockmen, if ever on some sunny day,
While tailing a mob, you should happen that way,
Tread light by the mound in the tall gum trees' shade,
For it may be the spot where our comrade is laid.

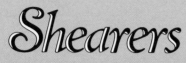

Shearers

At first the stockmen and drovers looked down on the lowly shearer humping his bluey from station to station looking for work. Early shearers were usually itinerant labourers, convicts or freed convicts, shearing where they could on the primitive farms and stations, sometimes without even the shelter of a rough bush shed. But as the years passed, shearing became more organised, and the shearers more skilled; fencing spread, and more and more of the big cattle runs were turned over to sheep. Stockmen, who usually preferred to work cattle, bemoaned the change, and none better than 'Breaker' Morant in 'Since the Country Carried Sheep'. The balance of power between drovers and shearers began to shift, and the 'gun' shearer or 'ringer', the best in the shed, stole much of the drover's glamour. As the sheep stations grew, so did the size of the sheds. Some had 50 or more stands to handle the tens of thousands of sheep a squatter might have to shear in a season.

Shearers worked hard, and fought hard for their rights in the great shearers' strikes of the 1890s. Perhaps they were successful unionists because unlike the more solitary bush occupations, shearing relied on team work and encouraged a certain camaraderie. Although shearers might have tramped the tracks between sheds alone or with a mate, during shearing they lived and worked closely together, and each worker relied on the others to keep the wool flowing from sheep to shearer to classer and on to presser via the shed hands, rouseabouts and pickers-up who carried, swept, and skirted fleeces. Combs and cutters were kept sharp by an expert, and the tar-boy administered tar to the wounds of cut sheep.

If we can believe the ballads, many shearers tramped only as far as the nearest pub when they finished a shed. There they 'blew' their wages on booze and women, before trudging on to the next shed with empty pockets and a massive hang-over.

Shearers still have their own lore and language, still tell slanderous stories about their cooks, and resist the introduction of women into the sheds either professionally or as observers.

The women who work as shearers or wool classers or rouseabouts today would have had an even harder time of it years ago if 'The Banks of the Condamine' is to be believed: 'The squatters have given orders, love, No woman should do so' says Billy when Nancy suggests she accompany him shearing, using her 'delicate constitution' as an excuse. Henry Lawson's super in 'The Shearing Shed' says politely, 'The ladies are coming,' but there's a good chance that what he might have said was, 'Ducks on the pond!' — the traditional shearers' warning of approaching women.

Today shearers drive from shed to shed, or get a lift with the mail truck, and it's much easier to shear a 'century' (a hundred sheep) with machines than it was with hand shears. But the work is still back-breaking, and there's the same air of excitement in the sheds when shearing is in full swing.

I Don't Go Shearing Now

Walter William Head, 'John Drayman'

So you're off to Riverina, where the sun is shining clear,
And ewes and lambs are bleating, calling shearers far and near;
Where the musterers are busy and the grass is waving high,
And the July fogs are climbing up the sunbeams to the sky;
Where the trefoil and the crowfoot in the pens are growing rank,
And the mud is getting sun-cracked on the falling river's bank;
Where the cook is in possession and the teams are carting wood,
And they're patching up the oven — which was never understood —
And the carpenters are fixing up the gates and pens and bins,
While the pressers, just to kill time, press in bales the winter's skins.
And those cranky little grindstones, in the centre hollow-ground,
How they used to jump and wobble as you turned the handles round!
Has the boss stuck to his promise, putting new ones in their place,
Not too soft and not too gritty, broad and level on the face?
I've been there, you know, my sonny, and I know exactly how
Those grindstones hurt your feelings — though I don't go shearing
    now . . .

You'll be wondering what old faces will be missing from the shed
For some are shearing elsewhere and some perhaps are dead.
And each succeeding muster you will notice with a sigh
That some old friends are missing — and you vaguely wonder why,
And where they're shearing this year. Ah, I know exactly how
These little things affect you — though I don't go shearing now . . .

Then the start! — you're all excitement as you slowly feel your way,
And there isn't any hurry, as it takes you all the day
To get the sweet-lips going, and the boss severely damns
The mercenary mouser who opens on the rams,
For all are strangely awkward while the hands are getting in,
And it spoils a good beginning if you chip both wool and skin.
But the next day things have altered, and the short, hoarse,
    'Wool away!'
Replaces reminiscent jokes and latest leary lay;
The learners' awkward struggling, at which all hands had laughed,
Forgotten is as silently you settle down to graft —
Each man his neighbour watching, noting each the other's pace,
As you move a little faster, feeling fitter for the race.
If you find from those about you that you're gaining more and more,
Then you take to watching others, faster men along the floor;
And as the speed grows greater you will find that not a few
Are anxiously, discreetly, on the quiet, watching you.
So the pace goes on increasing and the sweat begins to drop,
Every man has found his pacer and is going at his top;
But ere many days are over weak ones fall back one by one
Hit by chips and bullets flying from the boss's little gun;
I've been there, you know, my sonny, and I know exactly how
The fight gets fairly started — though I don't go shearing now . . .

Shedwards silent figures flitting in the dawning cold and grey,
Then a rush at ringing signal, all together — fire away!
Laboured breathing, bodies straining, painfully you turn and twist,
Small blows first, then open wider as the stiffness leaves your wrist.
There's the flying hurry-scurry up and down the greasy floors
Of the pickers and the broomies; there's the banging of the doors
And the rattle of the wool-press with its hard metallic din,
And the hoof-taps on the battens when the ewes and lambs rush in.
'Wool away!' and 'Tar!' and 'Sheep-ho!' — sundry growls at
    clumsy boys —
Are excluded from the rule of 'No unnecessary noise'.
Ever constant, ever struggling, straining o'er the astonished brutes,
Too surprised to raise a protest till they're shorn and down
    the shoots.
Three smart rubs with well-oiled turkey, dab the shears in
    water-pot,
Rush away to catch another — thus doth rage the battle hot;
While the perspiration, streaming from the ringer as he swings
Round the jumbuck in a circle, splashes on the board in rings.
Smoke-ho! Sharpen; cobble drivers; file your knockers down
    at night; —
Off again with rush and rattle, shear-blades buried out of sight
'Neath the snowy fleeces falling, tumbling o'er like crests of foam —
Ah, my lad! 'tis little wonder that you love to northward roam
When the battle is beginning; for I know exactly how
Such a fight affects your feelings — though I don't go shearing
    now . . .

27

Since the Country Carried Sheep

Harry Morant, 'The Breaker'

We trucked the cows to Homebush, saw the girls, and started back,
Went West through Cunnamulla, and got to the Eulo track,
Camped a while at Gonybibil — but, Lord! you wouldn't know
It for the place where you and Mick were stockmen long ago.

Young Merino bought the station, fenced the run and built a 'shed',
Sacked the stockmen, sold the cattle, and put on sheep instead,
But he wasn't built for Queensland; and every blessed year
One hears of 'labour troubles' when Merino starts to shear.

There are ructions with the rouseabouts, and shearers' strikes
    galore!
The likes were never thought of in the cattle days of yore.
And slowly, round small paddocks now, the 'sleeping lizards' creep,
And Gonybibil's beggared since the country carried sheep.

Time was we had the horses up ere starlight waned away,
The billy would be boiling by the breaking of the day;
And our horses — by Protection — were aye in decent nick,
When we rode up the 'Bidgee where the clearskins mustered thick.
They've built *brush-yards* on Wild Horse Creek, where in the
    morning's hush
We've sat silent in the saddle, and listened for the rush
Of the scrubbers — when we heard 'em, 'twas wheel 'em if you can,
While gidgee, pine and mulga tried the nerve of horse and man.

The mickies that we've branded there! the colts we had to ride!
In Gonybibil's palmy days — before the old boss died.
Could Yorkie Hawkins see his run, I guess his ghost would weep,
For Gonybibil's beggared since the country carried sheep.

From sunrise until sunset through the summer days we'd ride,
But stockyard rails were up and pegged, with cattle safe inside,
When 'twixt the gloamin' and the murk, we heard the well-known
    note —
The peal of boisterous laughter from the kookaburra's throat.

Camped out beneath the starlit skies, the tree-tops overhead,
A saddle for a pillow, and a blanket for a bed,
'Twas pleasant, mate, to listen to the soughing of the breeze,
And learn the lilting lullabies which stirred the mulga-trees.

Our sleep was sound in those times, for the mustering days
    were hard,
The morrows might be harder, with the branding in the yard.
But did you see the station now! the men — and mokes — they keep!
You'd own the place was beggared — since the country carried
    sheep.

Bluey Brink

There once was a shearer by name, Bluey Brink,
A devil for work and a devil for drink;
He'd shear his two hundred a day without fear,
And drink, without stopping, two gallons of beer!

When the pub opened up, he was very first in,
Roaring for whisky and howling for gin;
Saying — 'Jimmy, me boy, I'm dying with thirst,
Whatever you've got here, just give to me first.'

Now, Jimmy, the barman who served out the rum,
Hated the sight of old Bluey the bum;
He stayed far too late and he came much too soon —
At morning, at evening, at night and at noon!

One morning, while Jimmy was cleaning the bar
With sulphuric acid he kept in a jar,
He poured out a measure into a small glass,
Saying, 'After this drink, your will surely say "Pass!" '

Says Bluey to Jimmy, 'This stuff it tastes fine,
She's a new kind of liquor, not whisky or wine?
Yes, that's the stuff, Jimmy, I'm strong as a Turk —
I'll break all the records today at me work!'

Well, all that day long, there was Jim at the bar,
And he was consumed with a terrible fear;
Too worried to argue, too anxious to fight,
Seeing that shearer a corpse in his fright!

But early next morn, Bluey came as before;
Roaring and bawling and howling for more;
His eyeballs all singed and his whiskers deranged,
He had holes in his hide like a dog with the mange!

Said Bluey to Jimmy, 'That sure was fine stuff,
It made me feel well but I ain't had enough!
It started me coughing, well, you know I'm no liar,
But every damn cough set me whiskers on fire!'

The Shearing Shed

Henry Lawson

'The ladies are coming,' the super says
To the shearers sweltering there,
And 'the ladies' means in the shearing-shed:
'Don't cut 'em too bad. Don't swear.'
The ghost of a pause in the shed's rough heart,
And lower is bowed each head;
And nothing is heard, save a whispered word,
And the roar of the shearing-shed.

The tall, shy rouser has lost his wits,
And his limbs are all astray;
He leaves a fleece on the shearing-board,
And his broom in the shearer's way.
There's a curse in store for that jackeroo
As down by the wall he slants —
But the ringer bends with his legs askew
And wishes he'd 'patched them pants'.

They are girls from the city. Our hearts rebel
As we squint at their dainty feet,
While they gush and say in a girly way
That 'the dear little lambs' are 'sweet'.
And Bill, the ringer, who'd scorn the use
Of a childish word like 'damn',
Would give a pound that his tongue were loose
As he tackles a lively lamb.

Swift thoughts of homes in the coastal towns —
Or rivers and waving grass —
And a weight on our hearts that we cannot define
That comes as the ladies pass.
But the rouser ventures a nervous dig
With his thumb in the next man's back;
And Barcoo says to his pen-mate: 'Twig
The style of the last un, Jack.'

Jack Moonlight gives her a careless glance —
Then he catches his breath with pain —
His strong hand shakes and the sunbeams dance
As he bends to his work again.
But he's well disguised in a bristling beard,
Bronzed skin, and his shearer's dress;
And whatever he knew or hoped or feared
Was hard for his mates to guess.

Jack Moonlight, wiping his broad, white brow,
Explains, with a doleful smile:
'A stitch in the side,' and 'I'm all right now' —

But he leans on the beam awhile,
And gazes out in the blazing noon
On the clearing, brown and bare —
She has come and gone, like a breath of June,
In December's heat and glare.

The bushmen are big rough boys at the best,
With hearts of a larger growth;
But they hide those hearts with a brutal jest,
And the pain with a reckless oath.
Though the Bills and Jims of the bush-bard sing
Of their life loves, lost or dead.
The love of a girl is a sacred thing
Not voiced in a shearing-shed.

Ballad of 1891

The price of wool was falling in eighteen-ninety-one,
The men who owned the acres, saw something must be done;
'We will break the shearers' union, and show we're masters still;
And they'll take the terms we give them, or we'll find the men
     who will!'

From Clermont to Barcaldine, the shearers' camps were full;
Ten thousand blades were ready to strip the greasy wool;
When, through the west, like thunder, rang out the union's call —
'The sheds'll be shore union, or they won't be shore at all!'

O, Billy Lane was with them — his words were like a flame;
The flags of blue above them, they spoke Eureka's name.
'Tomorrow,' said the squatters, 'you'll find it does not pay —
We're bringing up free labourers to get the clip away!'

'Tomorrow,' said the shearers, 'they may not be so keen,
We can mount three thousand horsemen to show them what we
     mean!
Then we'll pack the west with troopers, from Bourke to Charters
     Towers —
You can have your fill of speeches, but the final strength is ours!'

'Be damned to your six-shooters, your troopers and police;
The sheep are growing heavy, the burr is in the fleece!
Then, if Nordenfeldt and Gatling won't bring you to your knees,
We'll find a law,' the squatters said, 'that's made for times like
     these!'

To trial at Rockhampton, the fourteen men were brought,
The judge had got his orders — the squatters owned the court!
But, for every one was sentenced, a thousand won't forget —
Where they gaol a man for striking, it's a rich man's country yet!

Down the River

Barcroft Boake

Hark, the sound of it drawing nearer,
Clink of hobble and brazen bell;
Mark the passage of stalwart shearer,
Bidding Monaro soil farewell.

Where is he making for? Down the river,
Down the river with eager tread;
Where is he making for? Down the river,
Down the river to seek a 'shed'.

Where is his dwelling on old Monaro?
Buckley's Crossing, or Jindaboine?
Dry Plain is it, or sweet Bolaira?
P'raps 'tis near where the rivers join
Where is he making for? Down the river,
When, oh when, will he turn him back?
Soft sighs follow him down the river,
Moist eyes gaze at his fading track.

See, behind him his pack-horse, ambling,
Bears the weight of his master's kit,
Oft and oft from the pathway rambling,
Crops unhampered by cruel bit.
Where is he making for? Equine rover,
Sturdy nag from the Eucumbene,
Tempted down by the thought of clover,
Springing luscious in Riverine.

Dreams of life and its future chances,
Snatch of song to beguile the way;
Through green crannies the sunlight glances,
Silver-gilding the bright 'Jack Shay'.
'So long, mate, I can stay no longer,
So long, mate, I've no time to stop;
Pens are waiting me at Mahonga,
Bluegong, Grubben and Pullitop.

'What! you say that the river's risen?
What! that the melted snow has come?
What! that it locks and bars our prison?
Many's the mountain stream I've swum.
I must onward and cross the river,
So long, mate, for I cannot stay;
I must onward and cross the river,
Over the river there lies my way.'

One man short when the roll they're calling,
One man short at old Bobby Rand's;

Heads are drooping and tears are falling
Up on Monaro's mountain lands.

Where is he making for? Down the river,
Down the river of slimy bed;
Where is he making for? Down the river,
Down the river that bears him, dead.

Click Go the Shears

Out on the board the old shearer stands
Grasping his shears in his thin bony hands;
Fixed is his gaze on a bare-bellied yeo —
Glory, if he gets her won't he make the ringer go.

Click go the shears, boys, click, click, click;
Wide is his blow and his hands move quick.
The ringer looks around and is beaten by a blow
And curses the old snagger with the bare-bellied yeo.

In the middle of the floor, in his cane-bottomed chair,
Sits the boss of the board with his eyes everywhere
Notes well each fleece as it comes to the screen
Saying, 'By the living Harry, can't you take 'em off clean?'

The tar-boy is there and awaiting in demand,
With his blackened tar-pot in his tarry hand.
Sees one old sheep with a cut upon its back —
Here is what he's waiting for — it's 'Tar here, Jack'.

Shearing is all over and we've all got our cheques
Roll up your swags, boys, we're off on the tracks.
The first pub we come to, it's there we'll have a spree,
And, everyone that comes along, it's 'Come and drink with me'.

Down by the bar, the older shearer stands
Grasping his glass in his thin bony hands
Fixed is his gaze on a green-painted keg
Glory, he'll get down on it before he stirs a leg.

There we leave him standing, shouting for all hands
Whilst, all around him, every shooter stands.
His eyes are on the cask which now is low'ring fast,
He works hard, he drinks hard, and goes to hell at last.

The Boss of the Shearing Shed

When I was young, I used to roam, for I was hard as nails;
I humped my swag along the track in sunny New South Wales.
I followed all the dusty roads, where'er my fancy led,
And that was how I came to meet the boss of the shearing shed.

He made us work the whole day long on a board all wet with slime;
And when I stopped to blow me nose, he said I was wasting time!
So, I grabbed his prize merino ram, and I slipped and cut its head —
And that was how I got the sack from the boss of the shearing shed.

Then, sadly I rolled up my swag and started down the track,
And there I met a pretty girl, a-mounted on a hack;
I asked the lass who she might be, and this is what she said —
'Why, Sir, I am the daughter of the boss of the shearing shed!'

Well, soon I found I loved that girl, and it was plain to see
By the twinkle in her pretty eyes, she'd took a shine to me!
One day, we wandered off to town, and there we two were wed;
And now I am the son-in-law of the boss of the shearing shed!

Springtime Brings on the Shearing

Oh, the springtime it brings on the shearing,
And it's then you will see them in droves,
To the west-country stations all steering,
A-seeking a job of the coves.

With a ragged old swag on my shoulder
And a billy quart-pot in my hand;
I'll tell you we'll 'stonish the new-chums
To see how we travel the land!

From billabong, Murray and Loddon,
To the far Tattiara and back;
The hills and the plains are well trodden
By the men of the wallaby track.

And after the shearing is over,
And the wool season's all at an end;
It is then you will see those flash shearers
Making johnny-cakes round in the bend.

Flash Jack From Gundagai

I've shore at Burrabogie, and I've shore at Toganmain,
I've shore at big Willandra and upon the old Coleraine,
But before the shearin' was over I've wished myself back again
Shearin' for old Tom Patterson, on the One-Tree Plain.

All among the wool, boys,
Keep your wide blades full, boys,
I can do a respectable tally myself when I like to try,
But they know me round the backblocks as Flash Jack from
*   Gundagai.*

I've shore at big Willandra and I've shore at Tilberoo,
And once I drew my blades, my boys, upon the famed Barcoo,
At Cowan Downs and Trida, as far as Moulamein,
But I always was glad to get back again to the One-Tree Plain.

I've pinked 'em with the Wolseleys and I've rushed with B-bows, too
And shaved 'em in the grease, my boys, with the grass seed showing
    through.
But I never slummed my pen, my lads, whate'er it might contain,
While shearin' for old Tom Patterson, on the One-Tree Plain.

I've been whalin' up the Lachlan, and I've dossed on Cooper's Creek,
And once I rung Cudjingie shed, and blued it in a week.
But when Gabriel blows his trumpet, lads, I'll catch the morning
    train,
And I'll push for old Tom Patterson's on the One-Tree Plain.

One of the Has-beens

I'm one of the has-beens, a shearer I mean,
I once was a ringer and used to shear clean,
I could make the wool roll off like the soil from the plough,
But you may not believe me 'cause I can't do it now.

I'm as awkward as a new chum and I'm used to the frown
That the boss often shows me, saying 'Keep those blades down'.

I've shorn with Pat Hogan, Bill Bright and Jack Gunn,
Charlie Fergus, Tommy Layton and the great roaring Dunn.
They brought from the Lachlan the best they could find,
But not one among them could leave me behind.

But it's no use complaining, I'll never say die,
Though the days of fast shearing for me have gone by;
I will take the world easy, shear slowly and clean,
And I merely have told you just what I have been.

The Banks of the Condamine

Oh, hark the dogs are barking, love,
I can no longer stay,
The men are all gone mustering
And it is nearly day.
And I must off by the morning light
Before the sun doth shine,
To meet the Sydney shearers
On the banks of the Condamine.

Oh, Billy, dearest Billy,
I'll go along with you,
I'll cut off all my auburn fringe
And be a shearer, too,
I'll cook and count your tally, love,
While ringer-o you shine,
And I'll wash your greasy moleskins
On the banks of the Condamine.

Oh, Nancy, dearest Nancy,
With me you cannot go,
The squatters have given orders, love,
No woman should do so;
Your delicate constitution
Is not equal unto mine,
To stand the constant tigering
On the banks of the Condamine.

Oh Billy, dearest Billy,
Then stay back home with me,
We'll take up a selection
And a farmer's wife I'll be:
I'll help you husk the corn, love,
And cook your meals so fine
You'll forget the ram-stag mutton
On the banks of the Condamine.

Oh, Nancy, dearest Nancy,
Please do not hold me back,
Down there the boys are waiting,
And I must be on the track;
So here's a good-bye kiss, love,
Back home here I'll incline
When we've shore the last of the jumbucks
On the banks of the Condamine.

The Lime Juice Tub

When shearing comes lay down your drums,
Step on the board, you brand new chums,
With a rah-dum rah-dum rub-a-dub-dub
We'll send you home in a lime juice tub.

Here we are in New South Wales,
Shearing sheep as big as whales,
With leather necks and dirty tails,
And fleece as tough as rusty nails.

The cockies' sons and brand new chums,
All fancy that they are great guns;
They fancy they can shear the wool
But the beggars can only tear and pull.

The very next job they undertake
Is to press the wool but they make a mistake,
They press the wool without any bales
Oh, shearing's hell in New South Wales.

And when with tar the sheep are black
Roll up, roll up; you'll get the sack,
Once more, once more on the wallaby track
Once more to look for work outback.

And when they meet upon the road
From off their backs they down their load,
And at the sun they take a look
And they reckon it's time to breast the cook.

You cockies too you never need fret
For to show you what I'll never forget
The kind of man who's willing to bet
You're up to your necks, heels first, in debt.

You're up to your necks, for all your sins,
Your daughters wear no crinolines
Nor are they troubled by boots or shoes,
For they're wild in the bush with the kangaroos.

We camp in huts without any doors,
Sleep upon the dirty floors
With a pannikin of flour and a sheet of bark
We can wallop on the damper in the dark.

Oh, home, it's home, I'd like to be
Not lumping my bluey in the sheep country,
Over a thousand miles I've come
To march along with a blanket drum.

'Ard Tack

I'm a shearer, yes I am, and I've shorn 'em, sheep and lamb,
From the Wimmera to the Darling Downs and back;
And I've rung a shed or two when the fleece was tough as glue,
But I'll tell you where I struck the 'ardest tack.

I was down round Yenda way, killin' time from day to day
Till the big sheds started movin' further out,
When I struck a bloke by chance that I summed up in a glance
As a cocky from a vineyard round about.

Now, it seems he picked me too, well, it wasn't 'ard to do
'Cos I 'ad some tongs a-hangin' from me hip;
'I got a mob,' he said, 'a mob about two hundred head,
And I'd give a ten-pun note to have the clip.'

I says, 'Right, I'll take the stand' (it meant gettin' in me 'and!)
And be nine o'clock we'd rounded up the mob;
In a shed sunk in the ground — yeah, with wine casks all around!
And that was where I started on me job.

I goes easy for a bit, while me 'and was gettin' fit,
And, by dinner-time, I'd done some 'arf a score;
With the cocky pickin' up and 'andin' me a cup
Of pinkie, after every sheep I shore!

The cocky 'ad to go away about the seventh day,
After showin' me the kind a' casks to use;
Then I'd do the pickin' up and manipulate the cup
Strollin' round the wine casks, just to pick and choose!

Then I'd stagger to the pen, grab a sheep and start again,
With a noise between a hiccup and a sob;
And sometimes I'd fall asleep with me arms around the sheep,
Worn and weary from me over-arduous job!

And so six weeks went by, until one day, with a sigh,
I pushed the dear old cobbler through the door,
Gathered in the cocky's pay, then staggered on me way
From the 'ardest bloody shed I ever shore.

Shearers

Henry Lawson

No church-bell rings them from the Track
No pulpit lights their blindness —
'Tis hardship, drought, and homelessness
That teach those Bushmen kindness:
The mateship born, in barren lands,
Of toil and thirst and danger,
The camp-fare for the wanderer set,
The first place to the stranger.

They do the best they can today —
Take no thought of the morrow;
Their way is not the old-world way —
They live to lend and borrow.
When shearing's done and cheques gone wrong,
They call it 'time to slither!' —
They saddle up and say 'So-long!'
And ride the Lord knows whither.

And though he may be brown or black,
Or wrong man there, or right man,
The mate that's steadfast to his mates
They call that man a 'white man!'
They tramp in mateship side by side —
The Protestant and Roman —
They call no biped lord or sir,
And touch their hat to no man!

They carry in their swags, perhaps,
A portrait and a letter —
And, maybe, deep down in their hearts,
The hope of 'something better'.
Where lonely miles are long to ride,
And long, hot days recurrent,
There's lots of time to think of men
They might have been — but weren't.

They turn their faces to the west
And leave the world behind them
(Their drought-dry graves are seldom set
Where even mates can find them).

They know too little of the world
To rise to wealth or greatness:
But in these lines I gladly pay
My tribute to their straightness.

The Albury Ram

As I was going to Albury,
Along the other day,
I met the finest sheep, sir,
That ever was fed on hay.

Indeed, sir, it's true, sir
I never was known to lie,
And, if you'd been to Albury,
You'd have seen the same as I!

The sheep he had four feet, sir,
Upon which he used to stand,
And every one of them, sir,
It covered an acre of land!

The sheep he had two horns, sir,
They grew so mighty wide,
They're going to build a bridge
With them from Dandenong to Clyde!

The sheep he had a tail, sir,
It grew so mighty long,
'Twas used to build a telegraph
From Sydney to Geelong!

The wool upon his belly,
It bore him off the ground,
'Twas sold in Melbourne the other day,
For a hundred thousand pounds!

The wool upon his back, sir,
It grew up to the moon;
The shearers went up in September,
And didn't get back till June!

The mutton that ram made, sir,
Gave all the army meat,
And what was left, I'm told, sir,
Was served up to the fleet!

The man who owned this sheep, sir,
He must have been mighty rich,
And the man who made this song up,
Was a lying son-of-a-gun!

There never was such a ram, sir,
It's all a terrible lie,
He's the biggest liar in Christendom,
Now YOU know it as well as I!

The Ryebuck Shearer

I come from the south and my name it's Field,
And when my shears are properly steeled,
A hundred and odd I have very often peeled,
And of course I'm a ryebuck shearer.

If I don't shear a tally before I go,
My shears and stone in the river I'll throw,
I'll never open Sawbees to take another blow,
And prove I'm a ryebuck shearer.

There's a bloke on the board and I heard him say
That I couldn't shear a hundred sheep a day,
But some fine day I'll show him the way,
And prove I'm a ryebuck shearer.

Oh, I'll make a splash, but I won't say when,
I'll hop off me tail and I'll into the pen,
While the ringer's shearing five, I'll shear ten,
And prove I'm a ryebuck shearer.

There's a bloke on the board and he's got a yellow skin,
A very long nose and he shaves on the chin,
And a voice like a billy-goat dancing on a tin,
And of course he's a ryebuck shearer.

Jog Along Till Shearing

The truth, it's in my song so clear,
Without a word of gammon:
The swagmen travel all the year
Waiting for the lambin'.
Now when this dirty work is done,
To the nearest shanty steering,
They meet a friend, their money spend,
Then jog along till shearing.

Home sweet home,
That is what they left it for,
Their home sweet home.

Now when the shearing season comes,
They hear the price that's going;
New arrivals meet old chums,
Then they start their blowing.
They say that they can shear each day
Their hundred pretty handy,
But eighty sheep is no child's play
If the wool is dense and sandy.

Now when the sheds are all cut out,
They get their bit of paper;
To the nearest pub they run
To cut a dashing caper.

They call for liquor plenty
And they're happy while they're drinking,
But where to go when the money's done
It's little they are thinking.

Sick and sore next morning,
They are when they awaken.
To have a drink of course they must
To keep their nerves from shakin'.
They call for one and then for two
In a way that's rather funny,
Till the landlord says, 'Now, this won't do;
You men have got no money.'

They're sleeping on verandahs
And they're lounging on the sofas;
For to finish up their spree
They're ordered off as loafers.
They've got no friends, their money's gone,
And at their disappearing,
They give three cheers for the river bends,
Then jog along till shearing.

Waiting for the Rain

The weather has been warm for a fortnight now or more,
And the shearers have been driving might and main,
For some have got the century who ne'er got it before,
But now we all are waiting for the rain.

For the boss is getting rusty and the ringer's caving in,
His bandaged wrist is aching with the pain;
And the second man, I fear, will make it hot for him.
Unless we have another fall of rain.

Now some had taken quarters and were keeping well in bunk
When we shore the six-tooth wethers from the plain.
And if the sheep get harder, then a few more men will flunk,
Unless we have another fall of rain.

Some cockies come here shearing, they would fill a little book
About this sad dry weather for the grain;
But here is lunch a-coming, make way for Dick the cook,
Old Dick is nigh as welcome as the rain.

But the sky is clouding over, and the thunder's muttering loud,
And the clouds are sweeping westward o'er the plain,
And I see the lightning flashing round the edge of yon black cloud,
And I hear the gentle patter of the rain.

So, lads, put up your stoppers, and let us to the hut,
Where we'll gather round and have a friendly game,
While some are playing music and some play ante up,
And some are gazing outwards at the rain.

But now the rain is over, let the pressers spin the screw,
Let the teamsters back their wagons in again,
We'll block the classer's table by the way we push them through.
For everything goes merry since the rain.

And the boss he won't be rusty when his sheep they all are shore,
And the ringer's wrist won't ache much with the pain
Of pocketing his cheque for a hundred quid or more,
And the second man will press him hard again.

Lazy Harry's

We started down from Roto when the sheds had all cut out,
With a three-spot cheque between us that we meant to push about,
But we passed the local boozer, we had Sydney in our eye,
Till we came to Lazy Harry's on the road to Gundagai.

Oh we came to Lazy Harry's on the road to Gundagai,
The road to Gundagai, not five miles from Gundagai,
We came to Lazy Harry's on the road to Gundagai.

We crossed the Murrumbidgee near the Yanco in a week,
And we passed through Old Narrandera and crossed the Burnett
 Creek,
But we never stopped at Wagga, we had Sydney in our eye,
Till we came to Lazy Harry's on the road to Gundagai.

Well, we strode into the parlour, threw our swags upon the floor,
And we ordered rum and raspberry and a shillin'-y cigar,
But the girl that served the poison, well she winked at Bill and I,
So we camped at Lazy Harry's on the road to Gundagai.

I've met a lot of girls, my boys, and drunk a lot of beer,
And met with some of both, my lads, that left me feeling queer,
But for grog to knock you sideways and for girls to make you sigh,
You should camp at Lazy Harry's on the road to Gundagai.

In a week the spree was over and the cheque was all knocked down,
So we shouldered our matildas and we turned our backs on town,
And the girls they stood a nobbler as we sadly said goodbye,
Then we tramped from Lousy Harry's on the road to Gundagai.

Shearin' in the Bar

My shearin' days are over, though I never was a gun;
I could always count my twenty at the end of every run;
I used the old 'Trade Union' shears, and the blades were always full
As I drove 'em to the knockers and I chopped away the wool.
I shore at Goorianawa and I didn't get the sack,
From Breeze out to Compadore, I always could get back!
And, though I am a truthful man, I find, when in a bar,
My tallies seem to double, but I never call for tar!

Shearin' on the western plains where the fleece is full of sand,
And the clover-burr and corkscrew-grass is the place to try your
    hand;
For the sheep are tall and wiry where they feed on the Mitchell
    grass,
And every second one of them is close to the cobbler class;
And a pen chock-full of cobblers is a shearer's dream of hell —
So, loud and lurid are their words when they catch one on the bell;
But, when we're pourin' down the grog, you'll have no call for tar,
For a shearer never cuts 'em when he's shearin' in a bar!

At Louth, I caught the ball-sheep, a wrinkled, tough-woolled brute,
Who never stopped his kicking till I tossed him down the chute;
My wrist was aching badly, but I fought him all the way —
Couldn't afford to miss a blow — I must earn my pound-a-day!
So, when I'd take a strip of skin, I'd hide it with my knee,
Turn the sheep around a bit where the right-bower couldn't see;
Then try and catch the rousie's eye and softly whisper, 'Tar';
But it never seems to happen when I'm shearin' in a bar!

Bonny Jess

Now the shearing time is over, Bonny Jess,
And the sheep are in the clover, Bonny Jess;
By the creek the cattle are lowing,
And the golden crops are growing,
While the setting sun is glowing, Bonny Jess,
And a kiss for you I'm throwing, Bonny Jess.

To your face the crimson's rushing, Bonny Jess,
And I know why you are blushing, Bonny Jess;
'Tis the memory appearing
Of the promise in the clearing,
When you said 'twixt hope and fearing, Bonny Jess,
You would wed me after shearing, Bonny Jess.

And now shearing time is over, Bonny Jess,
You are looking for your lover, Bonny Jess,
And my horse's hooves are ringing,
As along the road I'm swinging,
And a song for you I'm singing, Bonny Jess,
And the wedding ring I'm bringing, Bonny Jess.

Horses and Riders

Horses and Riders

There have been some legendary rides and riders in Australian folklore, and horses are still taken so seriously that a stuffed racehorse is one of the most popular exhibits in Melbourne's museum. Not surprisingly, some of the best bush balladists were riders. Barcroft Boake left the city to work as a boundary rider and drover; 'Banjo' Paterson grew up in the bush and moved to the city, but his love and understanding of horses never left him. Explorer and poet Ernest Favenc must have relied on horses in his expeditions or during his years working on stations in north Queensland. The Scot, Will Ogilvie, was drawn to Australia by his love of horses and his admiration for the horseman's poet Adam Lindsay Gordon, spending years working as a drover or breaking horses. Harry Morant won his nickname, 'The Breaker', through his skill and daring as a rider and horse-breaker. But the finest horseman was Adam Lindsay Gordon, whose daring feats were topped by his famous Blue Lake Leap, when he jumped his horse over a four-rail fence onto a small ledge of rock over 60 metres above the water of the famous lake just outside Mount Gambier in South Australia.

Horses and famous or unlikely rides are the subject of some of Australia's most popular stories, poems and ballads. A few are collected here in this chapter and throughout the rest of the book.

A Word to Texas Jack

Henry Lawson

Texas Jack, you are amusin'. By Lord Harry, how I laughed
When I seen yer rig and saddle with its bulwarks fore-and-aft;
Holy smoke! In such a saddle how the dickens can yer fall?
Why, I seen a gal ride bareback with no bridle on at all!
Gosh! so-help-me! strike-me-balmy! if a bit o' scenery
Like ter you in all yer rig-out on the earth I ever see.
How I'd like ter see a bushman use yer fixins, Texas Jack,
On the remnant of a saddle he can ride to hell and back.
Why, I heerd a mother screamin' when her kid went tossin' by
Ridin' bareback on a bucker that had murder in his eye.

What? yer come to learn the natives how to squat on horse's back!
Learn the cornstalk ridin'! Blazes! — w'at yer giv'n us, Texas Jack?
Learn the cornstalk — what the flamin', jumptup! where's my
      country gone?
Why, the cornstalk's mother often rides the day afore he's born!

You talk about your ridin' in the city, bold an' free,
Talk o' ridin' in the city, Texas Jack but where'd yer be
When the stock horse snorts an' bunches all 'is quarters in a hump,
And the saddle climbs a sapling, an' the horse-shoes split a stump?

No, before yer teach the native you must ride without a fall
Up a gum or down a gully nigh as steep as any wall —
You must swim the roarin' Darlin' when the flood is at its height
Bearin' down the stock an' stations to the Great Australian Bight.

You can't count the bulls an' bisons that yer copped with your
      lasso —
But a stout old myall bullock p'raps 'ud learn yer somethin' new;
Yer'd better make yer will an' leave yer papers neat an' trim
Before yer make arrangements for the lassoin' of *him*;
Ere you 'n 'yer horse is catsmeat, fittin' fate for sich galoots,
And yer saddle's turned to laces like we put in blucher boots.

And yer say yer death on Injins! We've got somethin' in yer line —
If yer think your fitin's ekal to the likes of Tommy Ryan.
Take yer karkass up to Queensland where the allygators chew
And the carpet-snake is handy with his tail for a lasso;
Ride across the hazy regins where the lonely emus wail
An' ye'll find the black'll track yer while yer lookin' for his trail;
He can track yer without stoppin' for a thousand miles or more —
Come again and he will show yer where yer spit the year before.
But yer'd best be mighty careful, you'll be sorry you kem here
When yer skewered to the fakements of yer saddle with a spear —
When the boomerang is sailin' in the air, may heaven help yer.
It will cut yer head off goin', an' come back again and skelp yer.

P.S. — As poet and as Yankee I will greet you, Texas Jack,
For it isn't no ill-feelin' that is gettin' up my back,
But I won't see this land crowded by each Yank and British cuss
Who takes it in his head to come a-civilisin' us.
So if yer feel like shootin' now, don't let yer pistol cough
(Our Government is very free at chokin' fellers off);
And though on your great continent there's misery in the towns
An' not a few untitled lords and kings without their crowns,
I will admit your countrymen is busted big, an' free,
An' great on ekal rites of men and great on liberty;
I will admit yer fathers punched the gory tyrant's head,
But then we've got our heroes too, the diggers that is dead —
The plucky men of Ballarat who toed the scratch right well,
And broke the nose of Tyranny and made his peepers swell
For yankin' Lib's gold tresses in the roarin' days gone by,
An' doublin' up his dirty fist to black her bonny eye;
So when it comes to ridin' mokes, or hoistin' out the Chow,
Or stickin' up for labour's rights, we don't want showin' how.

They come to learn us cricket in the days of long ago,
An' Hanlan come from Canada to learn us how to row,
An' 'doctors' come from 'Frisco just to learn us how to skite
An' 'pugs' from all the lands on earth to learn us how to fight;
An' when they go, as like or not, we find we're taken in,
They've left behind no larnin' — but they've carried off our tin.

The Man From Snowy River

A. B. 'Banjo' Paterson

There was movement at the station, for the word had passed around
That the colt from old Regret had got away,
And had joined the wild bush horses — he was worth a thousand
    pound,
So all the cracks had gathered to the fray,
All the tried and noted riders from the stations near and far
Had mustered at the homestead overnight,
For the bushmen love hard riding where the wild bush horses are,
And the stockhorse snuffs the battle with delight.

There was Harrison, who made his pile when Pardon won the cup,
The old man with his hair as white as snow;
But few could ride beside him when his blood was fairly up —
He would go wherever horse and man could go.
And Clancy of the Overflow came down to lend a hand,
No better horseman ever held the reins;
For never horse could throw him while the saddle girths would
    stand,
He learnt to ride while droving on the plains.

And one was there, a stripling on a small and weedy beast,
He was something like a racehorse undersized,
With a touch of Timor pony — three parts thoroughbred at least —
And such as are by mountain horsemen prized.
He was hard and tough and wiry — just the sort that won't
    say die —
There was courage in his quick impatient tread;
And he bore the badge of gameness in his bright and fiery eye,
And the proud and lofty carriage of his head.

But still so slight and weedy, one would doubt his power to stay,
And the old man said, 'That horse will never do
For a long and tiring gallop — lad, you'd better stop away,
Those hills are far too rough for such as you.'
So he waited sad and wistful — only Clancy stood his friend —
'I think we ought to let him come,' he said;
'I warrant he'll be with us when he's wanted at the end,
For both his horse and he are mountain bred.

'He hails from Snowy River, up by Kosciusko's side,
Where the hills are twice as steep and twice as rough,
Where a horse's hoofs strike firelight from the flint stones every
    stride,
The man that holds his own is good enough.
And the Snowy River riders on the mountains make their home,
Where the river runs those giant hills between;
I have seen full many horsemen since I first commenced to roam,
But nowhere yet such horsemen have I seen.'

So he went — they found the horses by the big mimosa clump —
They raced away towards the mountain's brow,
And the old man gave his orders, 'Boys, go at them from the jump,
No use to try for fancy riding now.
And, Clancy, you must wheel them, try and wheel them to the right.
Ride boldly, lad, and never fear the spills,
For never yet was rider that could keep the mob in sight,
If once they gain the shelter of those hills.'

So Clancy rode to wheel them — he was racing on the wing
Where the best and boldest riders take their place,
And he raced his stockhorse past them, and he made the ranges ring
With the stockwhip, as he met them face to face.
Then they halted for a moment, while he swung the dreaded lash,
But they saw their well-loved mountain full in view,
And they charged beneath the stockwhip with a sharp and sudden
    dash,
And off into the mountain scrub they flew.

Then fast the horsemen followed, where the gorges deep and black
Resounded to the thunder of their tread,
And the stockwhips woke the echoes, and they fiercely answered
    back
From cliffs and crags that beetled overhead.
And upward, ever upward, the wild horses held their way,
Where mountain ash and kurrajong grew wide;
And the old man muttered fiercely, 'We may bid the mob good day,
No man can hold them down the other side.'

When they reached the mountain's summit, even Clancy took a pull,
It well might make the boldest hold their breath,
The wild hop scrub grew thickly, and the hidden ground was full
Of wombat holes, and any slip was death.
But the man from Snowy River let the pony have his head,
And he swung his stockwhip round and gave a cheer,
And he raced him down the mountain like a torrent down its bed,
While the others stood and watched in very fear.

He sent the flint stones flying, but the pony kept his feet,
He cleared the fallen timber in his stride,
And the man from Snowy River never shifted in his seat —
It was grand to see that mountain horseman ride.
Through the stringybarks and saplings, on the rough and broken
    ground,
Down the hillside at a racing pace he went;
And he never drew the bridle till he landed safe and sound,
At the bottom of that terrible descent.

He was right among the horses as they climbed the further hill,
And the watchers on the mountain standing mute,
Saw him ply the stockwhip fiercely, he was right among them still,
As he raced across the clearing in pursuit.
Then they lost him for a moment, where two mountain gullies met

In the ranges, but a final glimpse reveals
On a dim and distant hillside the wild horses racing yet,
With the man from Snowy River at their heels.

And he ran them single-handed till their sides were white with foam.
He followed like a bloodhound on their track,
Till they halted cowed and beaten, then he turned their heads for
    home,
And alone and unassisted brought them back.
But his hardy mountain pony he could scarcely raise a trot,
He was blood from hip to shoulder from the spur;
But his pluck was still undaunted, and his courage fiery hot,
For never yet was mountain horse a cur.

And down by Kosciusko, where the pine-clad ridges raise
Their torn and rugged battlements on high,
Where the air is clear as crystal, and the white stars fairly blaze
At midnight in the cold and frosty sky,
And where around The Overflow the reed beds sweep and sway
To the breezes, and the rolling plains are wide,
The man from Snowy River is a household word today,
And the stockmen tell the story of his ride.

The Outlaw and The Rider

He had come to Umarella when the drought of '98
Had made Monara Plains a sea of sand,
And the philanthropic super, taking pity on his state,
Had given him a start as extra hand.

No doubt he'd been a wonder, for at night he'd sit for hours,
And boast of marvellous feats he'd seen and done,
How he'd won the Axeman's Trophy at the Show in Charters
    Towers,
And had killed a Syrian hawker just for fun.

How he rung the shed at Blackall, beating Howe by thirty sheep,
He'd broken outlaw horses in at night,
And in seven rounds at Gympie put O'Sullivan to sleep
With a blow for which he had the patent right.

Now we had a horse, an outlaw, bred on Umarella run,
No fiercer colt had ever stretched the reins,
He had thrown Monara Billy and the station breaker, Dunne,
And was reckoned bad throughout the southern plains.

The Skipper came down strolling — we had planned the joke of
    course —
'I've letters here, must catch the mail,' he said;
'You had better take them, Jimmy, you can ride the chestnut horse,
But mind him or he'll have you on your head.'

Now, Jim threw on the saddle and the colt stood like a sheep
One moment and we thought our joke would fail,
But Jim was barely seated when the colt he gave a leap,
And went at it like a demon through the rails.

Down the lane we followed and we opened wide our eyes
To see Jim like a perfect horseman sit,
He would fetch the stockwhip round him every time the colt would
    rise,
And would tease him with the spurs whene'er he lit.

We made a rush for horses, down the lane we followed fast,
To see our outlaw thrashed was something new,
But when we reached the clump of trees where we had seen him
    last,
Both horse and man had disappeared from view.

For miles the track we followed, and for days we sought in vain,
All was bustle, horsemen riding here and there,
From the cattle camp on Kindra to the farms on Little Plain,
We searched the rugged country in despair.
The days to weeks had lengthened, still no tidings came to hand,
We felt all hope of finding them was lost,
Till a party searching eastward saw some footprints in the sand,
Showing plainly that a horse had lately crossed.

So we tracked along the hoof-marks where once deep grasses grew,
And on a flat hemmed in by gorges deep
We found that chestnut bucking still for all he ever knew,
And Jim was there astride him, fast asleep.

On the Range

Barcroft Boake

On Nungar the mists of the morning hung low,
The beetle-browed hills brooded silent and black,
Not yet warmed to life by the sun's loving glow,
As through the tall tussocks rode young Charlie Mac.
What cared he for mists at the dawning of day,
What cared he that over the valley stern 'Jack'
The monarch of frost, held his pitiless sway? —
A bold mountaineer, born and bred, was young Mac.

A galloping son of a galloping sire —
Stiffest fence, roughest ground, never took him aback;
With his father's cool judgement, his dash and his fire,
The pick of Monaro, rode young Charlie Mac.
And the pick of the stable the mare he bestrode —
Arab-grey, built to stay, lithe of limb, deep of chest,
She seemed to be happy to bear such a load
As she tossed the soft forelock that curled on her crest.

They crossed Nungar Creek, where its span is but short
At its head, where together spring two mountain rills,
When a mob of wild horses sprang up with a snort —
'By thunder!' quoth Mac, 'there's the Lord of the Hills.'

Decoyed from her paddock, a Murray-bred mare
Had fled to the hills with a warrigal band;
A pretty bay foal had been born to her there,
Whose veins held the very best blood in the land —
'The Lord of the Hills', as the bold mountain men,
Whose courage and skill he was wont to defy,
Had named him; they yarded him once, but since then
He'd held to the saying 'Once bitten twice shy.'

The scrubber, thus suddenly roused from his lair,
Struck straight for the timber with fear in his heart;
As Charlie rose up in his stirrups, the mare
Sprang forward, no need to tell Empress to start.
She laid to the chase just as soon as she felt
Her rider's skilled touch, light, yet firm, on the rein;
Stride for stride, lengthened wide, for the green timber belt,
The fastest half-mile ever done on the plain.

They raced to within half a mile of the bluff
That drops to the river, the squadron strung out.
'I wonder,' quoth Mac, 'has the bay had enough?'
But he was not left very much longer in doubt,
For the Lord of the Hills struck a spur for the flat
And followed it, leaving his mob, mares and all,
While Empress (brave heart, she could climb like a cat)
Down the stony descent raced with never a fall.

Once more did the Lord of the Hills strike a line
Up the side of the range, and once more he looked back,
So close were they now he could see the sun shine
In the bold grey eyes flashing of young Charlie Mac.

He saw little Empress, stretched out like a hound
On the trail of its quarry, the pick of the pack,
With ne'er-tiring stride, and his heart gave a bound
As he saw the lithe stockwhip of young Charlie Mac
Showing snaky and black on the neck of the mare
In three hanging coils with a turn round the wrist;
And he heartily wished himself back in his lair
'Mid the tall tussocks beaded with chill morning mist.

In his terror the brumby struck down the rough falls
T'wards Yiack, with fierce disregard for his neck —
'Tis useless, he finds, for the mare overhauls
Him slowly, no timber could keep her in check.

There's a narrow-beat pathway that winds to and fro
Down the deeps of the gully, half hid from the day,
There's a turn in the track, where the hop-bushes grow
And hide the grey granite that crosses the way
While sharp swerves the path round the boulder's broad base —
And now the last scene in the drama is played:
As the Lord of the Hills, with the mare in full chase,
Swept towards it, but, ere his long stride could be stayed,
With a gathered momentum that gave not a chance
Of escape, and a shuddering, sickening shock,
He struck on the granite that barred his advance
And sobbed out his life at the foot of the rock.

Then Charlie pulled off with a twitch on the rein,
And an answering spring from his surefooted mount,
One might say, unscathed, though a crimsoning stain
Marked the graze of the granite, but that would ne'er count
With Charlie, who speedily sprang to the earth
To ease the mare's burden, his deft-fingered hand
Unslackened her surcingle, loosened tight girth,
And cleansed with a tussock the spur's ruddy brand.

There he lay by the rock — drooping head, glazing eye,
Strong limbs stilled for ever; no more would he fear
The tread of a horseman; no more would be fly
Through the hills with his harem in rapid career,
The pick of the Mountain Mob, bays, greys, or roans.
He proved by his death that the place 'tis that kills,
And a sun-shrunken hide o'er a few whitened bones
Marks the last resting-place of the Lord of the Hills.

The Little Worn-out Pony

There's a little worn-out pony this side of Hogan's shack
With a snip upon his muzzle and a mark upon his back;
Just a common little pony is what most people say,
But then of course they've never heard what happened in his day;
I was droving on the Leichhardt with a mob of pikers wild,
When this tibby little pony belonged to Hogan's child.

One night it started raining — we were camping on a rise,
When the wind blew cold and bleakly and thunder shook the skies;
The lightning cut the figure eight around the startled cattle,
Then down there fell torrential rains and then began a battle.
In a fraction of an instant the wild mob became insane,
Careering through the timber helter-skelter for the plain.

The timber fell before them like grass before a scythe,
And heavy rain in torrents poured from the grimly blackened sky;
The mob rushed ever onward through the slippery sodden ground,
While the men and I worked frantically to veer their heads around;
And then arose an awful cry — it came from Jimmy Rild,
For there between two saplings straight ahead was Hogan's child.

I owned not man or devil, I had not prayed since when,
But I called upon the blessed Lord to show His mercy then;
I shut my eyes and ground my teeth, the end I dared not see
Great God! The cattle — a thousand head — were crashing through
  the trees.
'God pity us bush children in our darkest hour of need,'
Were the words I prayed although I followed neither church or creed.

Then my right-hand man was shouting, the faithful Jimmy Rild,
'Did you see it, Harry, see the way he saved that child?'
'Saved! Saved, did you say?' and I shot upright with a bound,
'Yes, saved,' he said, 'indeed old man, the child is safe and sound.'
I was feeling pretty shaky and was gazing up the track,
Just then a pony galloped, the kid hopped on its back.

'A blinding flash of lightning then the thunder's rolling crack;
With two hands clasped upon his mane he raced towards the shack.'
'Good heavens, man,' I shouted then, 'if that is truly so,
To blazes with the cattle, to the shanty we must go.'
We reached Bill Hogan's shanty in fifteen minutes ride,
Then left our horses standing and wildly rushed inside.

The little child was there unhurt but shivering with fear,
And Hogan told us, 'Yes thank God, the pony brought her here.'

There's a little worn-out pony just this side of Hogan's shack
With a snip upon his muzzle and a mark upon his back;
Just a common little pony is what most people say,
But I doubt if there's his equal in the pony world today.

The Steeplechase Riders

We will deck them in cream and in crimson,
In chocolate and tartan and blue;
And speed them away from the barrier,
And trust them to battle it through.

Oh, the riders, the steeplechase riders;
They carry their lives in their hands.

We come with the best of our sportsmen,
And the fairest fair girls in the land,
To speed them away from the barrier
And cheer them in front of the stand.

For the fences are big ones and solid,
They make it top speed from the start;
And the men who ride out over Flemington
Need more than the average heart!

There's a roar from the crowd on the corner,
There's a shout from the crowd on the hill;
For the green and white hoops have turned over!
Loose horse and a man's lying still!

Oh, here's to the luck of the winner;
And here's better luck to the last;
Here's to their pluck at the timber,
And here's to the post flying past!

Old Bush Characters

48

Old Bush Characters

Many of the stars of 'Banjo' Paterson's ballads have become folk characters, known and loved by generations of Australians. Here are some of his most famous: 'The Man from Ironbark' with a throat as tough as leather; poor William Johnson whose terror of snakes turned his brain 'rather queer'; Maginnis Magee, victim of a tipsy priest; and Mulga Bill, named for his habitat — the mulga of the far outback — a noted horseman but an inadequate cyclist. Saltbush Bill, Clancy, and 'The Man from Snowy River' appear in other chapters. Some of them are innocents, but tough and determined nonetheless. Others have enough guile and gall to see them through any of the vicissitudes of bush life. All of them are unforgettable.

No other Australian poet quite matched the Banjo's ability to create memorable characters, but a few came close. Hartigan's whinging Hanrahan must come to many minds when faced with the soulful moans of 'rooned' farmers, and the method McDougall used to top the score is typical of the sharp practices of many of Banjo's characters.

But some old bush characters raise a tear as often as a laugh, and some of the ballads immortalise the loyalties, longings and suffering that formed the dark side of bush life: Henry Kendall's poem 'The Last of His Tribe' which bears witness to the genocide of the Aboriginal people; Moreton Bay — the 'lament' for the hated Captain Logan who was killed by an Aboriginal at the promptings of the convicts he had treated so cruelly; Lawson's touching but sentimental tributes to the sorrowing women left behind in the bush by the men they loved; and the poignant life and death of old Corney and his faithful dog.

Whether these characters make you laugh or cry, you are unlikely ever to forget them.

Johnson's Antidote

A. B. 'Banjo' Paterson

Down along the Snakebite River, where the overlanders camp,
Where the serpents are in millions, all of the most deadly stamp;
Where the station cook in terror, nearly every time be bakes,
Mixes up among the doughboys half a dozen poison snakes:
Where the wily free selector walks in armour-plated pants,
And defies the stings of scorpions, and the bites of bulldog ants:
Where the adder and the viper tear each other by the throat,
There it was that William Johnson sought his snakebite antidote.

Johnson was a free selector, and his brain went rather queer,
For the constant sight of serpents filled him with a deadly fear;
So he tramped his free selection, morning, afternoon and night,
Seeking for some great specific that would cure the serpent's bite.
Till King Billy, of the Mooki, chieftain of the flour bag head,
Told him, 'Spos'n snake bite pfeller, pfeller mostly drop down dead;
Spos'n snake bite old goanna, then you watch a while you see,
Old goanna cure himself with eating little pfeller tree.'
'That's the cure,' said William Johnson, 'point me out this plant
  sublime,'
But King Billy, feeling lazy, said he'd go another time.
Thus it came to pass that Johnson, having got the tale by rote,
Followed every stray goanna, seeking for the antidote.

* * *

Loafing once beside the river, while he thought his heart would
  break,
There he saw a big goanna, fighting with a tiger snake,
In and out they rolled and wriggled, bit each other, heart and soul,
Till the valiant old goanna swallowed his opponent whole,
Breathless, Johnson sat and watched him, saw him struggle up the
  bank,
Saw him nibbling at the branches of some bushes, green and rank;
Saw him, happy and contented, lick his lips, as off he crept,
While the bulging in his stomach showed where his opponent slept.
Then a cheer of exultation burst aloud from Johnson's throat;
'Luck at last,' said he, 'I've struck it! 'tis the famous antidote.

'Here it is, the Grand Elixir, greatest blessing ever known,
Twenty thousand men in India die each year of snakes alone.
Think of all the foreign nations, negro, chow, and blackamoor,
Saved from sudden expiration, by my wondrous snakebite cure.
It will bring me fame and fortune! In the happy days to be,
Men of every clime and nation will be round to gaze on me —
Scientific men in thousands, men of mark and men of note,
Rushing down the Mooki River, after Johnson's antidote.
It will cure *delirium tremens*, when the patient's eyeballs stare
At imaginary spiders, snakes which really are not there.

When he thinks he sees them wriggle, when he thinks he sees them
  bloat,
It will cure him just to think of Johnson's Snakebite Antidote.'

Then he rushed to the museum, found a scientific man —
'Trot me out a deadly serpent, just the deadliest you can;
I intend to let him bite me, all the risk I will endure,
Just to prove the sterling value of my wondrous snakebite cure.
Even though an adder bit me, back to life again I'd float;
Snakes are out of date, I tell you, since I've found the antidote.'

Said the scientific person, 'If you really want to die,
Go ahead — but, if you're doubtful, let your sheepdog have a try.
Get a pair of dogs and try it, let the snake give both a nip;
Give your dog the snakebite mixture, let the other fellow rip;
If he dies and yours survives him, then it proves the thing is good.
Will you fetch your dog and try it?' Johnson rather thought he would.
So he went and fetched his canine, hauled him forward by the
  throat.
'Stump, old man,' says he, 'we'll show them we've the genwine
  antidote.'

Both the dogs were duly loaded with the poison gland's contents;
Johnson gave his dog the mixture then sat down to wait events.
'Mark,' he said, 'in twenty minutes Stump'll be a-rushing round,
While the other wretched creature lies a corpse upon the ground.'
But, alas for William Johnson! ere they'd watched a half-hour's spell
Stumpy was as dead as mutton, t'other dog was live and well.
And the scientific person hurried off with utmost speed,
Tested Johnson's drug and found it was a deadly poison weed;
Half a tumbler killed an emu, half a spoonful killed a goat,
All the snakes on earth were harmless to that awful antidote.

* * *

Down along the Mooki River, on the overlanders' camp
Where the serpents are in millions, all of the most deadly stamp,
Wanders, daily, William Johnson, down among those poisonous
  hordes,
Shooting every stray goanna, calls them 'black and yaller frauds'.
And King Billy, of the Mooki, cadging for the cast-off coat,
Somehow seems to dodge the subject of the snakebite antidote.

Said Hanrahan

P. J. Hartigan, 'John O'Brien'

'We'll all be rooned,' said Hanrahan
In accents most forlorn
Outside the church ere Mass began
One frosty Sunday morn.

The congregation stood about,
Coat-collars to the ears,
And talked of stock and crops and drought
As it had done for years.

'It's lookin' crook,' said Daniel Croke;
'Bedad, it's cruke, me lad,
For never since the banks went broke
Has seasons been so bad.'

'It's dry, all right,' said young O'Neil,
With which astute remark
He squatted down upon his heel
And chewed a piece of bark.

And so around the chorus ran,
'It's keepin' dry, no doubt.'
'We'll all be rooned,' said Hanrahan,
'Before the year is out.

'The crops are done; ye'll have your work
To save one bag of grain;
From here way out to Back-o'-Bourke
They're singin' out for rain.

'They're singin' out for rain,' he said,
'And all the tanks are dry.'
The congregation scratched its head
And gazed around the sky.

'There won't be grass, in any case,
Enough to feed an ass;
There's not a blade on Casey's place
As I came down to Mass.

'If rain don't come this month,' said Dan,
And cleared his throat to speak —
'We'll all be rooned,' said Hanrahan,
'If rain don't come this week.'

A heavy silence seemed to steal
On all at this remark;
And each man squatted on his heel,
And chewed a piece of bark.

'We want an inch of rain, we do,'
O'Neil observed at last;
But Croke 'maintained' we wanted two
To put the danger past.

'If we don't get three inches, man,
Or four to break this drought,
We'll all be rooned,' said Hanrahan,
'Before the year is out.'

In God's good time down came the rain;
And all the afternoon
On iron roof and window-pane
It drummed a homely tune.

And through the night it pattered still,
And lightsome, gladsome elves
On dripping spout and window-sill
Kept talking to themselves.

It pelted, all day long,
A-singing at its work,
Till every heart took up the song
Way out to Back-o'-Bourke.

And every creek a banker ran,
And dams filled overtop;
'We'll all be rooned,' said Hanrahan,
'If this rain doesn't stop.'

And stop it did, in God's good time:
And spring came in to fold
A mantle o'er the hills sublime
Of green and pink and gold.

And days went by on dancing feet,
With harvest-hopes immense,
And laughing eyes beheld the wheat
Nid-nodding o'er the fence.

And oh, the smiles on every face,
As happy lad and lass
Through grass knee-deep on Casey's place
Went riding down to Mass.

While round the church in clothes genteel
Discoursed the men of mark,
And each man squatted on his heel,
And chewed his piece of bark.

'There'll be bushfires for sure, me man,
There will, without a doubt;
We'll all be rooned,' said Hanrahan,
'Before the year is out.'

The Squatter's Daughter

Henry Lawson

Out in the west, where runs are wide,
And days than ours are hotter,
Not very far from Lachlan Side
There dwelt a wealthy squatter.

Of old opinions he was full —
An Englishman, his sire,
Was hated long where peasants pull
Their forelocks to the squire.

He lov'd the good old British laws,
And Royalty's regalia,
And oft was heard to growl because
They wouldn't fit Australia.

This squatter had a lovely child —
An angel bright we thought her;
And all the stockmen rude and wild
Ador'd the squatter's daughter.

But on a bright eventful morn,
A swell of northern nation —
A lordling — brought his languid yawn
And eyeglass to the station.

He coveted the squatter's wealth;
He saw the squatter's daughter:
And, what is more than heart or health,
His empty title bought her.

And 'Yes', the father made her say
In spite of tears and kissing;
But early on the wedding day
The station found her missing.

And madder still the squatter grew,
And madder still the lover,
When by-and-by a-missing too,
A stockman they discover.

Then on the squatter's brow the frown
Went blacker still and blacker;
He sent a man to bring from town
A trooper and a tracker.

The dusty rascal saw the trail;
He never saw it plainer;
The reason why he came to fail
Will take a shrewd explainer.

A day and night the party lose;
The track the tracker parried;
And then a stockman brought the news —
'The runaways were married!'

The squatter swore that he'd forgive,
Perhaps, when he forgot her;
But he'd disown her while he'd live,
And while they called him squatter.

But as the empty months went o'er,
To ease his heart's vexation
He brought his bold young son-in-law
To manage stock and station.

And glad was he that he forgave,
Because a something had he
To keep his grey hairs from the grave,
And call him 'Dear Grand Daddy'.

To Democratic victories
In after years he'd listen;
And, strange to say, to things like these
His aged eyes would glisten.

The lordling took another girl
Not quite of his desire,
And went to where the farmers twirl
Their forelocks to the squire.

Now often to the station comes
An old and wrinkl'd tracker:
They cheer his heart with plenty rum,
And, 'plenty pheller bacca.'

Mulga Bill's Bicycle
A. B. 'Banjo' Paterson

'Twas Mulga Bill, from Eaglehawk, that caught the cycling craze;
He turned away the good old horse that served him many days;
He dressed himself in cycling clothes, resplendent to be seen;
He hurried off to town and bought a shining new machine;
And as he wheeled it through the door, with air of lordly pride,
The grinning shop assistant said, 'Excuse me, can you ride?'

'See here, young man,' said Mulga Bill, 'from Walgett to the sea,
From Conroy's Gap to Castlereagh, there's none can ride like me.
I'm good all round at everything, as everybody knows,
Although I'm not the one to talk — I *hate* a man that blows.
But riding is my special gift, my chiefest, sole delight;
Just ask a wild duck can it swim, a wildcat can it fight.
There's nothing clothed in hair or hide, or built of flesh or steel,
There's nothing walks or jumps, or runs, on axle, hoof, or wheel,
But what I'll sit, while hide will hold and girths and straps are tight:
I'll ride this here two-wheeled concern right straight away at sight.'

'Twas Mulga Bill, from Eaglehawk, that sought his own abode,
That perched above the Dead Man's Creek, beside the mountain
    road.
He turned the cycle down the hill and mounted for the fray,
But ere he'd gone a dozen yards it bolted clean away.
It left the track, and through the trees, just like a silver streak,
It whistled down the awful slope towards the Dead Man's Creek.

It shaved a stump by half an inch, it dodged a big white-box:
The very wallaroos in fright went scrambling up the rocks,
The wombats hiding in their caves dug deeper underground,
As Mulga Bill, as white as chalk, sat tight to every bound.
It struck a stone and gave a spring that cleared a fallen tree,
It raced beside a precipice as close as close could be;
And then as Mulga Bill let out one last despairing shriek
It made a leap of twenty feet into the Dead Man's Creek.

'Twas Mulga Bill, from Eaglehawk, that slowly swam ashore:
He said, 'I've had some narrer shaves and lively rides before;
I've rode a wild bull round a yard to win a five-pound bet,
But this was the most awful ride that I've encountered yet.
I'll give that two-wheeled outlaw best; it's shaken all my nerve
To feel it whistle through the air and plunge and buck and swerve.
It's safe at rest in Dead Man's Creek, we'll leave it lying still;
A horse's back is good enough henceforth for Mulga Bill.'

The Last of His Tribe
Henry Kendall

He crouches, and buries his face on his knees,
And hides in the dark of his hair;
For he cannot look up to the storm-smitten trees,
Or think of the loneliness there:
Of the loss and the loneliness there.

The wallaroos grope through the tufts of the grass,
And turn to their covers for fear;
But he sits in the ashes and lets them pass
Where the boomerangs sleep with the spear:
With the nullah, the sling, and the spear.

Uloola, behold him! The thunder that breaks
On the tops of the rocks with the rain,
And the wind which drives up with the salt of the lakes
Have made him a hunter again:
A hunter and fisher again.

For his eyes have been full with a smouldering thought;
But he dreams of the hunts of yore,
And of foes that he sought, and of fights that he fought
With those who will battle no more:
Who will go to the battle no more.

It is well that the water which tumbles and fills
Goes moaning and moaning along;
For an echo rolls out from the sides of the hills,
And he starts at a wonderful song:
At the sounds of a wonderful song.

And he sees, through the rents of the scattering fogs,
The corroboree warlike and grim,
And the lubra who sat by the fire on the logs,
To watch, like a mourner, for him:
Like a mother and mourner, for him.

Will he go in his sleep from these desolate lands,
Like a chief, to the rest of his race,
With the honey-voiced woman who beckons, and stands,
And gleams like a Dream in his face —
Like a marvellous Dream in his face?

The Shakedown on the Floor

Henry Lawson

Set me back for twenty summers —
For I'm tired of cities now —
Set my feet in red-soil furrows
And my hands upon the plough,
With the two 'Black Brothers' trudging
On the home stretch through the loam —
While, along the grassy siding,
Come the cattle grazing home.

And I finish ploughing early,
And I hurry home to tea —
There's my black suit on the stretcher,
And a clean white shirt for me;
There's a dance at Rocky Rises,
And, when all the fun is o'er,
For a certain favoured party
There's a shakedown on the floor.

You remember Mary Carey,
Bushmen's favourite at the Rise?
With her sweet small freckled features,
Red-gold hair, and kind grey eyes;
Sister, daughter, to her mother,
Mother, sister, to the rest —
And of all my friends and kindred,
Mary Carey loved me best.

Far too shy, because she loved me,
To be dancing oft with me;
What cared I, because she loved me,
If the world were there to see?
But we lingered by the sliprails
While the rest were riding home,
Ere the hour before the dawning,
Dimmed the great star-clustered dome.

Small brown hands that spread the mattress
While the old folk winked to see
How she'd find an extra pillow
And an extra sheet for me.
For a moment shyly smiling,
She would grant me one kiss more —
Slip away and leave me happy
By the shakedown on the floor.

Rock me hard in steerage cabins,
Rock me soft in wide saloons,
Lay me on the sand-hill lonely

Under waning western moons;
But wherever night may find me
Till I rest for evermore —
I will dream that I am happy
On the shakedown on the floor.

Ah! she often watched at sunset —
For her people told me so —
Where I left her at the sliprails
More than fifteen years ago.
And she faded like a flower,
And she died, as such girls do,
While, away in Northern Queensland,
Working hard, I never knew.

And we suffer for our sorrows,
And suffer for our joys,
From the old bush days when mother
Spread the shakedown for the boys.
But to cool the living fever,
Comes a cold breath to my brow,
And I feel that Mary's spirit
Is beside me, even now.

A Bush Christening

A. B. 'Banjo' Paterson

On the outer Barcoo where the churches are few,
And men of religion are scanty,
On a road never cross'd 'cept by folk that are lost,
One Michael Magee had a shanty.

Now this Mike was the dad of a ten-year-old lad,
Plump, healthy, and stoutly conditioned;
He was strong as the best, but poor Mike had no rest
For the youngster had never been christened.

And his wife used to cry, 'If the darlin' should die
Saint Peter would not recognise him.'
But by luck he survived till a preacher arrived,
Who agreed straightaway to baptise him.

Now the artful young rogue, while they held their collogue,
With his ear to the keyhole was listenin',
And he muttered in fright while his features turned white,
'What the divil and all is this christenin'?

He was none of your dolts, he had seen them brand colts,
And it seemed to his small understanding,
If the man in the frock made him one of the flock,
It must mean something very like branding.

So away with a rush he set off for the bush,
While the tears in his eyelids they glistened —
''Tis outrageous,' says he, 'to brand youngsters like me,
I'll be dashed if I'll stop to be christened!'

Like a young native dog he ran into a log,
And his father with language uncivil,
Never heeding the "praste" cried aloud in his haste,
'Come out and be christened, you divil!'

But he lay there as snug as a bug in a rug,
And his parents in vain might reprove him,
Till his reverence spoke (he was fond of a joke)
'I've a notion,' says he, 'that'll move him.

'Poke a stick up the log, give the spalpeen a prog;
Poke him aisy — don't hurt him or maim him,
'Tis not long that he'll stand, I've the water in hand,
As he rushes out this end I'll name him.

'Here he comes, and for shame! ye've forgotten the name —
Is it Patsy or Michael or Dinnis?'
Here the youngster ran out, and the priest gave a shout —
'Take your chance, anyhow, wid "Maginnis"!'

As the howling young cub ran away to the scrub
Where he knew that pursuit would be risky,
The Priest, as he fled, flung a flask at his head
That was labelled 'Maginnis's Whisky!'

And Maginnis Magee has been made a J. P.,
And the one thing he hates more than sin is
To be asked by the folk who have heard of the joke,
How he came to be christened 'Maginnis'!

The Great Northern Line

My love he is a teamster, a handsome man is he,
Red shirt, white moleskin trousers and hat of cabbage tree.
He drives a team of bullocks and whether it's wet or fine,
You will hear his whip a-cracking on the Great Northern Line.

Watch him, pipe him, twig him how he goes,
With his little team of bullocks he cuts no dirty shows,
He's one of the flash young carriers that on the road do shine,
With his little team of bullocks on the Great Northern Line.

And when he swings the greenhide he raises skin and hair,
His bullocks all have shrivelled horns, for Lordy he can swear;
But I will always love him, this splendid man of mine,
With his little team of bullocks on the Great Northern Line.

When he bogged at Mundowie and the bullocks took the yoke,
They strained their bellies on the ground until the bar chain broke,
He fixed it up with fencing wire and brought wool from Bundamine,
With his little team of bullocks on the Great Northern Line.

When he comes into Tamworth, you will here the ladies sigh,
And parents guard their daughters for he has a roving eye;
But he signals with his bullock whip as he comes through the pine,
With his little team of bullocks on the Great Northern Line.

My love he is a teamster, a handsome man is he,
Red shirt, white moleskin trousers and hat of cabbage tree.
And I will always love him, this splendid man of mine,
With his little team of bullocks on the Great Northern Line.

The Song of Old Joe Swallow

Henry Lawson

When I was up the country in the rough and early days,
I used to work along ov Jimmy Nowlett's bullick-drays;
Then the reelroad wasn't heeded of, an' the bush was wild an'
    strange,
An' we useter draw the timber from the saw-pits in the range —
Load provisions for the stations, an' we'd travel far and slow
Through the plains an' 'cross the ranges in the days o' long ago.

Then it's yoke up the bullicks and tramp beside 'em slow,
An' saddle up yer horses an' a-ridin' we will go,
To the bullick-drivin', cattle-drovin',
Nigger, digger, roarin', rovin'
Days o' long ago.

Once me and Jimmy Nowlett loaded timber for the town,
But we hadn't gone a dozen mile before the rain come down,
An' me and Jimmy Nowlett an' the bullicks an' the dray
Was cut off on some risin' ground while floods around us lay;
An' we soon run short of tucker an' terbacca, which was bad,
An' pertaters dipped in honey was the only tuck we had.

An' half our bullicks perished when the drought was on the land,
An' the burning heat that dazzles as it dances on the sand;
When the sun-baked clay an' gravel paves for miles the burnin'
    creeks,
An' at ev'ry step yer travel there a rottin' carcass reeks —
But we pulled ourselves together, for we never used ter know
What a feather bed was good for in those days o' long ago.

But in spite ov barren ridges an' in spite ov mud an' heat,
An' dust that browned the bushes when it rose from bullicks' feet,
An' in spite ov cold and chilblains when the bush was white with
    frost,
An' in spite of muddy water where the burnin' plain was crossed,
An' in spite of modern progress, and in spite of all their blow,
'Twas a better land to live in, in the days o' long ago.

When the frosty moon was shinin' o'er the ranges like a lamp,
An' a lot of bullick-drivers was a-campin' on the camp,
When the fire was blazin' cheery an' the pipes was drawin' well,
Then our songs we useter chorus an' our yarns we useter tell;
An' we'd talk ov lands we come from, and ov chaps we useter know,
For there always was behind us *other* days o' long ago.

Ah, them early days was ended when the reelroad crossed the plain,
But in dreams I often tramp beside the bullick-team again:
Still we pauses at the shanty just to have a drop er cheer,
Still I feels a kind ov pleasure when the campin'-ground is near;

Still I smells the old tarpaulin me an' Jimmy useter throw
O'er the timber-truck for shelter in the days o' long ago.

I have been a-driftin' back'ards with the changes ov the land,
An' if I spoke ter bullicks now they wouldn't understand,
But when Mary wakes me sudden in the night I'll often say:
'Come here, Spot, an' stan' up, Bally, blank an' blank an'
    come-eer-way.'
An' she says that, when I'm sleepin', oft my elerquince 'ill flow
In the bullick-drivin' language ov the days o' long ago.

Well, the pub will be soon be closin', so I'll give the thing a rest;
But if you should drop on Nowlett in the far an' distant west —
An' if Jimmy uses doubleyou instead of ar an' vee,
An' if he drops his aitches, then you're sure to know it's he.
An' yer won't forgit to arsk him if he still remembers Joe
As knowed him up the country in the days o' long ago.

Then it's yoke up the bullicks and tramp beside 'em slow,
An' saddle up yer horses an' a-ridin' we will go,
To the bullick-drivin', cattle-drovin',
Nigger, digger, roarin', rovin'
Days o' long ago.

The Squatter, Three Cornstalks, and the Well

(A DIRGE OF SIN AND SORROW,
SUNG BY JOE SWALLOW)
Henry Lawson

There was a Squatter in the land —
So runs the truthful tale I tell —
There also were three Cornstalks, and
There also was the Squatter's Well.

Singing *(Slowly):* 'Sin and sorrer, sin
and sor-rer, sin and sor-r-r-rer.'

The squatter he was full of pluck,
The Cornstalks they were full of sin,
The well it was half full of muck
That many rains had drifted in.

Singing *(with increased feeling)* 'Sin, etc.'

The Squatter hired the Cornstalks Three
To cleanse the well of mud and clay;
And so they started willing-lee
At five-and-twenty bob a day.

Singing *(apprehensively):* 'Sin, etc.'

At five-and-twenty bob the lot —
That's eight-and-four the day would bring
To each; and so they thought they'd got
A rather soft and easy thing.

Singing *(sadly):* 'Sin, etc.'

The Cornstalks cleaned the well within
A day or two, or thereabout —
And then they worked an awful sin —
A scheme to made the job last out.

Singing *(reproachfully):* 'Sin, etc.'

For when the well was cleaned out quite
Of all its logs and muck and clay
They tipped a drayload down at night
And worked to haul it up next day.

Singing *(dismally):* 'Sin, etc.'

But first the eldest, christened Hodge,
He greased the dray-wheel axles, so
The super wouldn't smell the dodge
And couldn't let the Squatter know.

Singing *(hopelessly):* 'Sin, etc.'

The stuff they surfaced out each day
With some surprise the Squatter saw.
He never dreamt the sand and clay
Was three miles off the night before.

Singing *(mournfully):* 'Sin, etc.'

But he got something in his eye,
It wasn't green, that's very plain.
He said the well was rather dry,
And they could fill it up again.

Singing *(mournfully and dismally):* 'Sin, etc.'

The Cornstalks went to work next day
In hope, of course, of extra tin —
The Squatter watched, and, sad to say,
The mullock wouldn't all go in.

Singing *(with great pathos):* 'Sin, etc.'

And tho' the Cornstalks twigged the ruse
Whereby the boss had done 'em brown,
They argued that the clay was loose,
And wanted time to settle down.
Singing *(hopelessly):* 'Sin, etc.'

The boss began to rave and tear,
And yelled with a most awful frown,
'I will not settle up, I swear,
Till that there clay is settled down!'

Singing *(hopefully):* 'Sin, etc.'

'Before my cheques yer'll pocket, boys,
Yer'll put a mountain in a well' —
The Cornstalks didn't make a noise,
They only murmured sadly — !

Singing *(triumphantly):* 'Sin, etc.'

Moral
There is a moral to my rhyme —
A moral to the dirge I sing —
That when you do go in for crime
You mustn't overdo the thing.

Singing *(more dismally than ever):*
'Sin and Sorrer, s-i-n- and sorr-r-r-rer!'

How McDougall Topped the Score

Thomas E. Spencer

A peaceful spot is Piper's Flat. The folk that live around —
They keep themselves by keeping sheep and turning up the ground;
But the climate is erratic, and the consequences are
The struggle with the elements is everlasting war.
We plough, and sow, and harrow — then sit down and pray for rain;
And then we all get flooded out and have to start again.
But the folk are now rejoicing as they ne'er rejoiced before
For we've played Molongo cricket, and McDougall topped the score!

Molongo had a head on it, and challenged us to play
A single-innings match for lunch — the losing team to pay.
We were not great guns at cricket, but we couldn't well say no,
So we all began to practise, and we let the reaping go.
We scoured the Flat for ten miles round to muster up our men,
But when the list was totalled we could only number ten.
Then up spoke big Tim Brady: he was always slow to speak,
And he said 'What price McDougall who lives down at
   Cooper's Creek?'

So we sent for old McDougall and he stated in reply
That he'd never played at cricket, but he'd half a mind to try.
He couldn't come to practise — he was getting in his hay,
But he guessed he'd show the beggars from Molongo how to play.
Now, McDougall was a Scotchman, and a canny one at that,
So he started in to practise with a paling for a bat.
He got Mrs Mac to bowl to him, but she couldn't run at all,
So he trained his sheep-dog, Pincher, how to scout and fetch the ball.

Now, Pincher was no puppy; he was old, and worn, and grey;
But he understood McDougall, and — accustomed to obey —
When McDougall cried out 'Fetch it!' he would fetch it in a trice,
But, until the word was 'Drop it!' he would grip it like a vice.
And each succeeding night they played until the light grew dim:
Sometimes McDougall struck the ball — sometimes the ball struck
   him.
Each time he struck, the ball would plough a furrow in the ground;
And when he missed, the impetus would turn him three times round.

The fatal day at length arrived — the day that was to see
Molongo bite the dust, or Piper's Flat knocked up a tree!
Molongo's captain won the toss, and sent his men to bat,
And they gave some leather-hunting to the men of Piper's Flat.

When the ball sped where McDougall stood, firm planted in his
   track,
He shut his eyes, and turned him round, and stopped it — with his
   back!
The highest score was twenty-two, the total sixty-six,
When Brady sent a yorker down that scattered Johnson's sticks.

Then Piper's Flat went in to bat, for glory and renown,
But, like the grass before the scythe, our wickets tumbled down.
'Nine wickets down for seventeen; with fifty more to win!'
Our captain heaved a heavy sigh, and sent McDougall in.
'Ten pounds to one you'll lose it!, cried a barracker from town';
But McDougall said 'I'll tak' it, mon!' and planked the money down.
Then he girded up his moleskins in a self-reliant style,
Threw off his hat and boots and faced the bowler with a smile.

He held the bat the wrong side out, and Johnson with a grin
Stepped lightly to the bowling crease, and sent a 'wobbler' in;
McDougall spooned it softly back, and Johnson waited there,
But McDougall, crying 'Fetch it!' started running like a hare.
Molongo shouted 'Victory! he's out as sure as eggs,'
When Pincher started through the crowd, and ran through
   Johnson's legs.
He seized the ball like lightning; then he ran behind a log,
And McDougall kept on running, while Molongo chased the dog!

They chased him up, they chased him down, they chased him round,
   and then
He darted through the sliprail as the scorer shouted 'Ten!'
McDougall puffed; Molongo swore; excitement was intense;
As the scorer marked down twenty, Pincher cleared a barbed-wire
   fence.

'Let us head him!' shrieked Molongo. 'Brain the mongrel with a bat!'
'Run it out! Good old McDougall!' yelled the men of Piper's Flat.
And McDougall kept on jogging, and then Pincher doubled back,
And the scorer counted 'Forty!' as they raced across the track.

McDougall's legs were going fast, Molongo's breath was gone —
But still Molongo chased the dog — McDougall struggled on.
When the scorer shouted 'Fifty' then they knew the chase could
   cease;
And McDougall gasped out 'Drop it!' as he dropped within the crease.

Then Pincher dropped the ball, and as instinctively he knew
Discretion was the wiser plan, he disappeared from view;
And as Molongo's beaten men exhausted lay around
We raised McDougall shoulder-high, and bore him from the ground.

We bore him to McGinniss's, where lunch was ready laid,
And filled him up with whisky-punch, for which Molongo paid.
We drank his health in bumpers and we cheered him three
   times three,
And when Molongo got its breath Molongo joined the spree.

And the critics say they never saw a cricket match like that,
When McDougall broke the record in the game at Piper's Flat,
And the folk are jubilating as they never did before;
For we played Molongo cricket — and McDougall topped the score!

The Man from Ironbark

A. B. 'Banjo' Paterson

It was the man from Ironbark who struck the Sydney town,
He wandered over street and park, he wandered up and down,
He loitered here, he loitered there, till he was like to drop.
Until at last in sheer despair he sought a barber's shop.
'Ere! shave my beard and whiskers off, I'll be a man of mark,
I'll go and do the Sydney toff up home in Ironbark.'

The barber man was small and flash, as barbers mostly are,
He wore a strike-your-fancy sash; he smoked a huge cigar;
He was a humorist of note and keen at repartee,
He laid the odds and kept a 'tote', whatever that may be,
And when he saw our friend arrive, he whispered, 'Here's a lark!
Just watch me catch him all alive, this man from Ironbark.'

There were some gilded youths that sat along the barber's wall.
Their eyes were dull, their heads were flat, they had no brains at all;
To them the barber passed the wink, his dexter eyelid shut,
'I'll make this bloomin' yokel think his bloomin' throat is cut.'
And as he soaped and rubbed it in he made a rude remark:
'I s'pose the flats is pretty green up there in Ironbark.'

A grunt was all reply he got; he shaved the bushman's chin,
Then made the water boiling hot and dipped the razor in.
He raised his hand, his brow grew black, he paused awhile to gloat,
Then slashed the red-hot razor-back across his victim's throat;
Upon the newly-shaven skin it made a livid mark —
No doubt it fairly took him in — the man from Ironbark.

He fetched a wild up-country yell might wake the dead to hear,
And though his throat, he knew full well, was cut from ear to ear,
He struggled gamely to his feet, and faced the murd'rous foe:
'You've done for me! you dog, I'm beat! one hit before I go!
I only wish I had a knife, you blessed murdering shark!
But you'll remember all your life the man from Ironbark.'

He lifted up his hairy paw, with one tremendous clout
He landed on the barber's jaw, and knocked the barber out.
He set to work with nail and tooth, he made the place a wreck;
He grabbed the nearest gilded youth, and tried to break his neck.
And all the while his throat he held to save his vital spark,
And 'Murder! Bloody murder!' yelled the man from Ironbark.

A peeler man who heard the din came in to see the show;
He tried to run the bushman in, but he refused to go.
And when at last the barber spoke, and said ''Twas all in fun —
'Twas just a little harmless joke, a trifle overdone.'
'A joke!' he cried, 'By George, that's fine; a lively sort of lark;
I'd like to catch that murdering swine some night in Ironbark.'

And now while round the shearing floor the list'ning shearers gape,
He tells the story o'er and o'er, and brags of his escape.
'Them barber chaps what keeps a tote, By George, I've had enough,
One tried to cut my bloomin' throat, but thank the Lord it's tough.'
And whether he's believed or no, there's one thing to remark,
That flowing beards are all the go way up in Ironbark.

Moreton Bay

One Sunday morning as I went walking
By Brisbane waters I chanced to stray,
I heard a convict his fate bewailing
As on the sunny river-bank he lay:

'I am a native of Erin's island,
Though banished now from my native shore;
They took me from my aged parents
And from the maiden whom I do adore.

'I've been a prisoner at Port Macquarie,
At Norfolk Island and Emu Plains,
At Castle Hill and at cursed Toongabbie,
At all those settlements I've worked in chains;
But of all places of condemnation
And penal stations in New South Wales
To Moreton Bay I have found no equal,
Excessive tyranny each day prevails.

'For three long years I've been beastly treated
And heavy irons on my legs I wore;
My back with flogging is lacerated
And often painted with my crimson gore.
And many a man from downright starvation
Lies mouldering now underneath the clay;
And Captain Logan he had us mangled
At the triangles of Moreton Bay.

'Like the Egyptians and ancient Hebrews
We were oppressed under Logan's yoke,
Till a native black lying there in ambush
Did deal our tyrant with his mortal stroke.
My fellow prisoners, be exhilarated
That all such monsters such death may find!
And when from bondage we are liberated
Our former sufferings shall fade from mind.'

Corney's Hut

Old Corney built in Deadman's Gap
A hut, where mountain shades grow denser,
And there he lived for many years,
A timber-getter and a fencer.
And no one knew if he'd a soul
Above long sprees or split-rail fences,
Unless, indeed, it was his dog
Who always kept his confidences . . .

If, as 'twas said, he was a swell
Before he sought these sombre ranges,
'Twixt mother's arms and coffin gear
He must have seen a world of changes.
But from his lips would never fall
A hint of home, or friends, or brothers,
And if he told his tale at all,
He must have told it as another's . . .

On New Year's Eve they found him dead —
For rum had made his life unstable —
They found him stretched upon his bed,
And also found, upon the table,
The coloured portrait of a girl —
Blue eyes of course. The hair was golden,
A faded letter and a curl,
And — well, we said the theme was olden.

The splitter had for days been dead
And cold before the sawyers found him,
And none had witnessed how he died
Except the dog who whimpered round him;
A noble friend, and of a kind
Who stay when other friends forsake us,
And he at last was left behind
To greet the rough bush undertakers . . .

'Ole Corney's dead,' the bushmen said;
'He's gone at last, an' ne'er a blunder.'
And so they brought a horse and dray
And tools to 'tuck the old cove under'.
The funeral wended through the range
And slowly round its rugged corners;
The reader will not think it strange
That Corney's dog was chief of mourners.

He must have thought the bushmen hard
And of his misery unheeding,
Because they shunned his anxious eyes
That seemed for explanation pleading.

At intervals his tongue would wipe
The jaws that seemed with anguish quaking;
As some strong hand impatiently
Might chide the tears for prison breaking.

They reached by rugged ways at last
A desolate bush cemetery,
Where now (our tale is of the past),
A thriving town its dead doth bury,
And where the bones of pioneers
Are found and thrown aside unheeded —
For later sleepers, blessed with tears
Of many friends, the graves are needed.

The funeral reached the bushmen's graves,
Where these old pioneers were sleeping,
And now while down the granite ridge
The shadow of the peak was creeping,
They dug a grave beneath a gum
And lowered the dead as gently may be,
As Corney's mother long before
Had laid him down to 'hush-a-baby'.

A bushman read the words to which
The others reverently listened,
Some bearded lips were seen to twitch,
Some shaded eyes with moisture glistened.
The boys had brought the splitter's tools,
And now they split and put together
Four panels such as Corney made,
To stand the stress of western weather.

'Old Corney's dead, he paid his bills,'
(These words upon the tree were graven),
'And oft a swagman down in luck
At Corney's mansion found a haven.'
But now the bushmen hurried on,
Lest darkness in the range should find them;
And strange to say they never saw
That Corney's dog had stayed behind them.

If one had thrown a backward glance
Along the rugged path they wended,
He might have seen a darker form
Upon the damp cold mound extended.
But soon their forms had vanished all,
And night came down the ranges faster,
And no one saw the shadows fall
Upon the dog that mourned his master.

Swaggies and Billabongs

Swaggies and Billabongs

In Australia's national song, our most famous swagman drowns himself in a billabong to avoid the squatter and troopers, perhaps not such an incomprehensible act when one considers that stock theft was a capital offence, and the swagman had one of the squatter's 'jumbucks' in his tucker bag. 'Banjo' Paterson is said to have recorded or written the words of 'Waltzing Matilda' on Dagworth station in Queensland after the manager's daughter showed him a billabong on the Diamantina where a swagman had drowned. The previous night she had played him the tune on the homestead piano.

Swagmen or swaggies take their name from the 'swag' they carried, a tight bundle usually containing a blue blanket (hence 'bluey' for swag), waterproof sheet, clothes, and a few personal belongings. From the swag hung food in a sugar bag, and a billy for making tea. Carrying a swag was called 'waltzing matilda', or 'humping the drum' or 'bluey'.

Swagmen were often wandering bushmen looking for work, unlike the sundowners, so named because they would turn up at a homestead for food and shelter at sundown, too late to do any work. In fact most itinerant bushmen and labourers would have been swagmen at some stage because few could afford other means of transport when times were really bad.

Most squatters provided food and shelter for the swagmen, willingly or not; those who did not soon found that the incidence of bushfires on their properties was far greater than on the properties of more generous neighbours! But the swagmen helped the squatters too by providing extra labour when it was needed, at shearing time, when there was fencing to be done, or the harvest to be brought in. But when the work was over, the swaggie would swing his bluey over one shoulder, thank the missus for the tucker she'd given him, and plod off along the wallaby track.

Waltzing Matilda

CARRYING A SWAG

A. B. 'Banjo' Paterson

Oh there once was a swagman camped in the billabongs,
Under the shade of a Coolibah tree;
And he sang as he looked at the old billy boiling,
'Who'll come a-waltzing Matilda with me.'

Who'll come a-waltzing Matilda, my darling,
Who'll come a-waltzing Matilda with me.
Waltzing Matilda and leading a water-bag,
Who'll come a-waltzing Matilda with me.'

Up came the jumbuck to drink at the waterhole,
Up jumped the swagman and grabbed him in glee;
And he sang as he put him away in his tucker-back,
'You'll come a-waltzing Matilda with me.'

Who'll come a-waltzing Matilda, my darling,
Who'll come a-waltzing Matilda with me.
Waltzing Matilda and leading a water-bag,
Who'll come a-waltzing Matilda with me.'

Up came the squatter a-riding his thoroughbred;
Up came policemen — one, two, and three.
'Whose is the jumbuck you've got in the tucker-bag?
You'll come a-waltzing Matilda with we.'

Who'll come a-waltzing Matilda, my darling,
Who'll come a-waltzing Matilda with me.
Waltzing Matilda and leading a water-bag,
Who'll come a-waltzing Matilda with me.'

Up sprang the swagman and jumped in the waterhole,
Drowning himself by the Coolibah tree;
And his voice can be heard as it sings in the billabongs,
'Who'll come a-waltzing Matilda with me.'

Who'll come a-waltzing Matilda, my darling,
Who'll come a-waltzing Matilda with me.
Waltzing Matilda and leading a water-bag,
Who'll come a-waltzing Matilda with me.'

The Reedy Lagoon

The sweet-scented wattle sheds perfume around,
Enticing the bird and the bee,
As I lie and take rest in a fern-covered nest
'Neath the shade of a kurrajong tree.
High up in the air I can hear the refrain
Of a butcher bird singing his tune,
For the spring in its glory has come back again
By the banks of the Reedy Lagoon.

I've carried my bluey for many a mile,
My boots are worn out at the toes,
And I'm dressing this season in quite different style,
From what I did last year, God knows.
My cooking utensils, I'm sorry to say,
Consist of a knife and a spoon;
And I've dry bread and tay in a battered Jack Shea
On the banks of the Reedy Lagoon.

O where is poor Franky, and couldn't he ride,
And Johnny, the kind-hearted boy?
They tell me that lately he's taken a bride,
A Benedick's life to enjoy.
And Mac the big Scotsman? I once heard him say
He wrestled the famous Muldoon.
But they're all far away and I'm lonely today
On the banks of the Reedy Lagoon.

O where is the lady I oft-times caressed,
The girl with the sad, dreamy eyes?
She pillows her head on another man's breast
Who tells her the very same lies.
My bed she would hardly be willing to share
Where I camp in the light of the moon.
But it's little I care for I couldn't keep square
On the banks of the Reedy Lagoon.

The Swagman and his Mate

Henry Lawson

From north to south throughout the year
The shearing seasons run,
The Queensland stations start to shear
When Maoriland has done;
But labour's cheap and runs are wide,
And some the track must tread
From New Year's Day till Christmastide
And never get a shed!
North, west, and south — south, west, and north —
They lead and follow Fate —
The stoutest hearts that venture forth —
The swagman and his mate.

A restless, homeless class they are
Who tramp in border land.
They take their rest 'neath moon and star —
Their bed the desert sand,
On sunset tracks they ride and tramp,
Till speech has almost died,
And still they drift from camp to camp
In silence side by side.
They think and dream, as all men do;
Perchance their dreams are great —
Each other's thoughts are sacred to
The swagman and his mate.

With scrubs beneath the stifling skies
Unstirred by heaven's breath;
Beyond the Darling Timber lies
The land of living death!
A land that wrong-born poets brave
Till dulled minds cease to grope —
A land where all things perish, save
The memories of Hope.
When daylight's fingers point out back
(And seem to hesitate)
The far faint dust cloud marks their track —
The swagman and his mate.

And one who followed through the scrub
And out across the plain,
And only in a bitter mood
Would see those tracks again; —
Can only write what he has seen —
Can only give his hand —
And greet those mates in words that mean
'I know', 'I understand'.
I hope they'll find the squatter 'white',

The cook and shearers 'straight',
When they have reached the shed to-night —
The swagman and his mate.

Out Back

Henry Lawson

The old year went, and the new returned, in the withering weeks of
  drought,
The cheque was spent that the shearer earned, and the sheds were
  all cut out;
The publican's words were short and few, and the publican's looks
  were black —
And the time had come, as the shearer knew, to carry his swag
  Out Back.

*For time means tucker, and tramp you must, where the scrubs and
  plains are wide,
With seldom a track that a man can trust, or a mountain peak to guide;
All day long in the dust and heat — when summer is on the track —
With stinted stomachs and blistered feet, they carry their swags Out
  Back.*

He tramped away from the shanty there, where the days were long
  and hot,
With never a soul to know or care if he died on the track or not.
The poor of the city have friends in woe, no matter how much they
  lack,
But only God and the swagmen know how a poor man fares Out
  Back.

He begged his way on the parched Paroo and the Warrego tracks
  once more,
And lived like a dog, as the swagmen do, till the Western stations
  shore;
But men were many, and sheds were full, for work in the town
  was slack —
The traveller never got hands in wool, though he tramped for a year
  Out Back.

In stifling noons when his back was wrung by its load, and the air
  seemed dead,
And the water warmed in the bag that hung to his aching arm
  like lead,
Or in times of flood, when plains were seas, and the scrubs were cold
  and black,
He ploughed in mud to his trembling knees, and paid for his sins
  Out Back.

He blamed himself in the year 'Too late' — in the heaviest hours
     of life —
'Twas little he dreamed that a shearing-mate had care of his home
     and wife;
There are times when wrongs from your kindred come, and
     treacherous tongues attack —
When a man is better away from home, and dead to the world,
     Out Back.

And dirty and careless and old he wore, as his lamp of hope
     grew dim;
He tramped for years till the swag he bore seemed part of himself
     to him.
As a bullock drags in the sandy ruts, he followed the dreary track,
With never a thought but to reach the huts when the sun went down
     Out Back.

It chanced one day, when the north wind blew in his face like a
     furnace-breath,
He left the track for a tank he knew — 'twas a short-cut to his death;
For the bed of the tank was hard and dry, and crossed with many a
     crack,
And, oh! it's a terrible thing to die of thirst in the scrub Out Back.

A drover came, but the fringe of law was eastward many a mile;
He never reported the thing he saw, for it was not worth his while.
The tanks are full and the grass is high in the mulga off the track,
Where the bleaching bones of a white man lie by his mouldering
     swag Out Back.

For time means tucker, and tramp they must, where the plains and
     scrubs are wide,
With seldom a track that a man can trust, or a mountain peak to guide;
All day long in the flies and heat the men of the outside track
With stinted stomachs and blistered feet must carry their swags
     Out Back.

The Sheepwasher's Lament

When first I took the Western track, the year was sixty-one,
The master was a worker then, the servant was a man;
But now the squatters, puffed with the pride, they treat us with
     disdain;
Lament with me the bygone days that will not come again.

With perfect health, a mine of wealth, the bushman stout and strong,
Would smoke his pipe and hum his tune, and sing his cheerful song,
But now we toil from morn till night, though much against the
     grain,
Lamenting on the bygone days that will not come again.

I once could boast two noble prads, to bear me on my way;
My good revolver in my belt, I never knew dismay.
But lonely now I hump my drum in sunshine and in rain,
Lamenting on the bygone days that will not come again.

I earned a decent cheque at times, and blued it like a lord,
My dress a prince's form would grace, and sprees I could afford.
But now in tattered rags arrayed, my limbs they ache with pain,
Lamenting on the bygone days that will not come again.

Let bushmen all in unity combine with heart and hand,
Till bloody cringing poverty is driven from our land;
Let never Queensland come to know the tyrant's ball and chain,
And workers all in time to come their vanished rights regain.

Wild Rover No More

I've been a wild rover this many a year,
And I've spent all my money on whisky and beer;
But now I'm returning with gold in great store,
And I never shall play the wild rover no more

No, no, never, never, no more,
I never shall play the wild rover no more.

There was Kitty and Betsy and Margaret and Sue,
And three or four more that belonged to our crew;
We'd sit up till morning and make the place roar;
I've been the wild boy but I'll be so no more.

Dropped into a shanty I used to frequent
And I told the landlady my money was spent,
I asked her for credit, she answered me, 'Nay,
Such a custom as yours I can get any day.'

Then I drew from my pocket ten sovereigns bright
And the landlady's eyes opened wide with delight.
Said she, 'I have whisky and wines of the best,
And the words that I told you were only in jest.'

I'll go home to my parents, confess what I've done,
And I'll ask them to pardon their prodigal son;
And if they will do so, as often before,
Then I never shall play the wild rover no more.

When Your Pants Begin to Go

Henry Lawson

When you wear a cloudy collar and shirt that isn't white,
And you cannot sleep for thinking how you'll reach tomorrow night,
You may be a man of sorrow, and on speaking terms with Care,
But as yet you're unacquainted with the Demon of Despair;
For I rather think that nothing heaps the trouble on your mind
Like the knowledge that your trousers badly need a patch behind.
I have noticed when misfortune strikes the hero of the play
That his clothes are worn and tattered in a most unlikely way;
And the gods applaud and cheer him while he whines and loafs
    around,
But they never seem to notice that his pants are mostly sound;
Yet, of course, he cannot help it, for our mirth would mock his care
If the ceiling of his trousers showed the patches of repair.

You are none the less a hero if you elevate your chin
When you feel the pavement wearing through the leather, sock and
    skin;
You are rather more heroic than are ordinary folk
If you scorn to fish for pity under cover of a joke;
You will face the doubtful glances of the people that you know;
But — of course, you're bound to face them when your pants
    begin to go.

If, when flush, you took your pleasure, failed to made a god of Pelf —
Some will say that for your troubles you can only thank yourself;
Some will swear you'll die a beggar, but you only laugh at that
While your garments hang together and you wear a decent hat;
You may laugh at their predictions while your soles are wearing
    through —
But a man's an awful coward when his pants are going too!

Though the present and the future may be anything but bright,
It is best to tell the fellows, that you're getting on all right.
And a man prefers to say it — 'tis a manly lie to tell,
For the folks may be persuaded that you're doing very well;
But it's hard to be a hero, and it's hard to wear a grin,
When your most important garment is in places very thin.

Get some sympathy and comfort from the chum who knows
    you best,
Then your sorrows won't run over in the presence of the rest;
There's a chum that you can go to when you feel inclined to whine,
He'll declare your coat is tidy, and he'll say 'Just look at mine!'
Though you may be patched all over he will say it doesn't show,
And he'll swear it can't be noticed when your pants begin to go.

Brother mine, and of misfortune! times are hard, but do not fret,
Keep your courage up and struggle, and we'll laugh at these
    things yet.

Though there is no corn in Egypt, surely Africa has some —
Keep your smile in working order for the better days to come!
We shall often laugh together at the hard times that we know.
And get measured by the tailor when our pants begin to go.

The Old Bark Hut

Oh, my name is Bob the swagman, and I'll have you understand
I've had my many ups and downs while travelling through the land;
I once was well-to-do, my lads, but now I'm so hard up
That I'm forced to go on rations in an old bark hut!

In an old bark hut, in an old bark hut,
(Repeat last line of each verse)

Ten pounds of flour, ten pounds of beef, some sugar and some tay,
That's all they give a hungry man until the seventh day!
If you don't be mighty sparing, you'll go with a hungry gut —
That's one of the great misfortunes of an old bark hut!

The bucket you boil your beef in has to carry water, too,
They'd say you're getting mighty flash if you should ask for two!
I've a billy and a pint-pot, and a broken-handled cup,
And they all adorn the table in the old bark hut.

Of furniture, there's no such thing — 'twas never in the place;
Except the stool I sit upon, and that's an old gin case;
I use if for a safe as well, but I must keep it shut,
Or the flies will make it canter round the old bark hut!

If you should leave it open, and the flies should find your meat,
They'll scarcely leave a single piece that's fit for a man to eat!
But you mustn't curse nor grumble — what won't fatten will fill up,
For what's out of sight is out of mind in an old bark hut!

In summer when the weather's warm, this hut is nice and cool;
You'll find the gentle breezes blowing in through every hole!
You can leave the old door open or you can leave it shut —
There's no fear of suffocation in the old bark hut!

In winter time, Lord bless my soul, to live in it's a treat,
Especially when it's raining hard and blowing wind and sleet!
The rain comes down the chimney and your meat gets black
    with soot —
That's a substitute for pepper in the old bark hut!

Beside my fire I make my bed, and there I lay me down;
And think myself as happy as a king that wears a crown;
But, as you're dozing off to sleep, the fleas will wake you up —
Which makes you curse the vermin in the old bark hut.

Miners
and Rushes

Miners and Rushes

The Victorian goldrush, which began in 1851, was the start of one of the most exciting periods in Australia's history. Gold was discovered in paying quantities in New South Wales in the 1860s, there was a rush to Queensland in 1875, and the last goldrush to Western Australia began in the 1890s. Migrants and visitors from all over the world flocked to the goldfields to try their luck. Despite the ethnic diversity of these people, they seemed to have had little effect on the dress, habits or culture on the fields, if the songs, ballads, stories or paintings of the time can be relied upon. The Chinese, who persisted with their oriental dress, habits and culture, were the only obvious exceptions to this. The rest seemed to take up the prevailing ethos with gusto, or like 'The Green New Chum' at least try to, so that the stereotypical white Australian male — a loyal mate who loved freedom and grog and hated the traps (police) and authority in general — continued to be the dominant type. The women on the goldfields seem to have been largely ignored in our literature; even Henry Lawson, whose redoubtable mother Louisa gave birth to him in a tent on the goldfields, concentrated on his fellow men.

On the Victorian fields especially there were plenty of traps for the diggers to hate, and good reason for their hatred. The sale of liquor on the goldfields was banned, the ban was strictly if unsuccessfully policed, and enormous licence fees were levied. Licence hunts were regular and ruthless, and police were often belligerent and corrupt. Informers such as the one in 'Laying Information' bedevilled the sly grog shops, where liquor of questionable quality was sold at exorbitant prices; informers were paid half the fines. Police tyranny eventually resulted in the miners' rebellion at the Eureka Stockade at Ballarat, immortalised in 'The Cross of the South'.

When the diggers weren't avoiding or fighting the traps, they worked hard, and only a very few were really lucky.

After the surface gold was exhausted, deep shafts had to be sunk, and the cry of 'Look out below!' echoed over the fields as the person operating the windlass let down the bucket. The very real danger to the person down the shaft is recorded in Lawson's poem 'Cameron's Heart'.

Life at the diggings wasn't always unremitting toil — in Bendigo and other large centres, first tents and then English style music-halls were erected to house entertainers, some of whom earned fabulous sums for performing for the diggers. One, an ex-digger Charles Thatcher, was extremely popular for his songs about the diggers' life, and many of his songs are still known today, sung to the melodies of old music-hall tunes.

Gold was not and is not the only precious substance mined in Australia, and there are still many people fossicking for gold, opals, precious metals or semi-precious stones whose life has not changed dramatically from the times of the first diggers.

A Yarn of Lambing Flat

'Call that a yarn!' said old Tom Pugh, 'What rot! I'll lay my hat
I'll sling a yarn worth more nor two such pumped-up yarns as that,'
And thereupon old Tommy 'slew' a yarn of Lambing Flat.

'When Lambing Flat broke out,' he said, ''mongst others there
  I knew
A lanky, orkard, Lunnon-bred young chap named Johnnie Drew,
And nicknamed for his love of bed the Sleeping Beauty too . . .

'A duffer-rush broke out one day, I quite forget where at —
(It doesn't matter, anyway, it didn't feed a cat) —
And Johnnie's party said they'd say good-bye to Lambing Flat.

'Next morn rose Johnnie's mates to pack and make an early shunt,
But all they could get out of Jack was 'All right', or a grunt,
By pourin' water down his back and — when he turned —
  his front . . .

'Well, arter that, I'm safe to swear, the beggars didn't lag,
But packed their togs with haste and care, and each one made
  his swag
With Johnnie's moleskins, every pair included in the bag.

'With nimble fingers from the pegs they soon the strings unbent,
And off its frame as sure as eggs they drew the blessed tent,
And rolled it up and stretched their legs, and packed the lot —
  and went.

'They sez as twelve o'clock was nigh — we'll say for sure eleven —
When Johnnie ope'd his right-hand eye and looked straight up to
  heaven:
I reckon he got more surprise than struck the fabled Seven.

'Clean off his bunk he made a bound, and when he rubbed his eyes
I'm safe to swear poor Johnnie found his dander 'gin to rise.
For there were diggers standin' round — their missuses likewise . . .

And in the sun that day Jack stood clad only in his shirt,
And fired with stones and bits of wood, and with his tongue threw
  dirt;
He fought as long as e'er he could — but very few were hurt.

'He stooped to tear a lump of schist out of the clinging soil,
By thunder you should heard him jist, and seen the way he'd coil
Upon the ground, and hug his fist, and scratch and dig and toil!

''Twas very plain he'd struck it fat, the dufferin' Lunnon muff:
The scoff and butt of Lambing Flat who always got it rough,
Could strike his fortune where he sat; the joker held the stuff.

'Well, that's the yarn, it ain't so poor: them golden days is o'er,
And Dublin Pat was drowned, and sure it quenched his thirst for
  gore;

Old Corney Bill and Dave the Cure I never heard of more.

'The Sleepin' Beauty's wealthy, too, and wears a shiny hat,
But often comes to old Tom Pugh to have a quiet chat;
I lent him pants to get him through his fix on Lambing Flat.'

The Cross of the South

'Twas the month of December, the year '54,
When the men of Eureka rebelled;
When they swore that the flag that they'd made for themselves
Hither proudly aloft would be held.
Oh, the miners took arms in the stockade that day,
The bold words passed from mouth to mouth —
'We will stand by this flag and the stars that she bears,
White stars of the Cross of the South.'

Though the hot blood of heroes ran fast in their veins,
There was but one man they obeyed!
And the hero of heroes they chose from their ranks,
Peter Lalor, their hero they made.
Peter Lalor said, 'Now you must stand by your guns,
Fear not the cannon's fierce mouth;
For I see that the soldiers are gathering now
To tear down the Cross of the South!'

Captain Thomas, he charged the Eureka Stockade
With three hundred troops by his side;
Fire and steel met them there and they fell back again,
But the first of the miners had died!
And the smoke of the battle had scarce cleared away,
When the soldiers came charging once more!
And the miners were killed as they stood round the flag,
Or fell from the wounds that they bore.

Bold Peter Lalor lay shot on the ground
Where the soldiers had left him for dead!
The flag that he loved lay there by his side,
The white stars all stained with red!
Peter Lalor, he rose on his knees in the dust,
These wild words poured from his mouth —
'You can murder us all in black tyranny's name,
But you can't kill the Cross of the South.'

The Rescue

Edward Dyson

There's a sudden, fierce clang of the knocker,
Then the sound of a voice in the shaft,
Shrieking words that drum hard on the centres,
And the braceman goes suddenly daft:
'Set the whistle a-blowing like blazes! Billy, run, give old Mackie a
    call —
Run, you fool! Number Two's gone to pieces,
And Fred Baker is caught in the fall!
Say, hullo! there below — any hope, boys, any chances of saving his
    life?'
'Heave away!' says the knocker. 'They've started.
God be praised, he's no youngsters or wife!'

Screams the whistle in fearful entreaty,
And the wild echo raves on the spur,
And the night, that was still as a sleeper
In soft, charmed sleep, is astir
With the fluttering of wings in the wattles,
And the vague, frightened murmur of birds,
With far cooees that carry the warning,
Running feet, inarticulate words.
From the black belt of bush come the miners,
And they gather by Mack on the brace,
Out of breath, barely clad, and half-wakened,
With a question in every face.

'Who's below?' 'Where's the fall?' 'Didn't I tell you —
Didn't I say that them sets wasn't sound?'
'Is it Fred? He was reckless with Baker;
Now he's seen his last shift underground.'
'And his mate? Where is Sandy McFadyn?'
'Sandy's snoring at home on his bunk.'
'Not at work! Name o' God! a foreboding?'
'A foreboding be hanged! He is drunk!'
'Take it steady there, lads!' the boss orders.
He is white to the roots of his hair.
'We may get him alive before daybreak
If he's close to the face and has air.'

In the dim drive with ardour heroic
Two facemen are pegging away.
Long and Coots in the rise heard her thunder,
And they fled without word or delay
Down the drive, and they rushed for the ladders,
And they went up the shaft with a run,
For they knew the weak spot in the workings,
And the guess there was graft to be done.
Number Two was pitch dark, and they scrambled

To the plat and they made for the face,
But the roof had come down fifty yards in,
And the reef was all over the place . . .

By the faint yellow glow of the candles,
Where the dank drive is hot with their breath,
On the verge of the Land of the Shadow,
Waging war breast to bosom with Death,
How they struggle, these giants! and slowly,
As the trucks rattle into the gloom,
Inch by inch they advance to the conquest
Of a prison — or is it a tomb?
And the workings re-echo a volley
As the timbers are driven in place;
Then a whisper is borne to the toilers:
'Boys, his mother is there on the brace!'

Like veterans late into action,
Fierce with longing to hew and to hack,
Riordan's shift rushes in to relieve them,
And the toil-stricken men stagger back.
'Stow the stuff, mates, wherever there's stowage!
Run the man on the brace till he drops!
There's no time to think on this billet!
Bark the heels of the trucker who stops!
Keep the props well in front, and be careful.
He's in there, and alive, never fret.'
But the grey dawn is softening the ridges, and
Word has not come to us yet.

Still the knocker rings out, and the engine
Shrieks and strains like a creature in pain
As the cage rushes up to the surface
And drops back into darkness again.
By the capstan a woman is crouching.
In her eyes neither hope nor despair;
But a yearning that glowers like frenzy
Bids those who'd speak pity forbear.
Like a figure in stone she is seated
Till the labour of rescue be done.
For the father was killed in the Phoenix,
And the son — Lord of pity! the son?

'Hullo! there on top!' they are calling.
'They are through! He is seen in the drive!'
They have got him — thank Heaven! they've got him,
And oh, blessed be God, he's alive!'
'Man on! heave away!' 'Step aside, lads;
Let his mother be first when he lands.'
She was silent and strong in her anguish;
Now she babbles and weeps where she stands,
And the stern men, grown gentle, support her

At the mouth of the shaft, till at last
With a rush the cage springs to the landing,
And her son's arms encircle her fast.

Laying Information

'Tis twelve at night, and there upon the camp,
A foot-policeman silent watch is keeping,
And thus he talks and chuckles to himself,
Whilst all his brother traps in bed are sleeping;
'The tents I'll stick up next I will not name,
But I'll go and take an observation,
And if they're green enough to sell me grog,
Why then I'll go and lay my information.'

The night is past, the sun resplendent shines,
As a digger then this trap himself disguises,
And then he goes into a sly-grog store,
Handles the things and asks their various prices;
He blithely talks about the Russian war,
Descants upon the policy of the nation,
And brings away a bottle of brown stout,
Then, coolly, goes and lays an information.

He enters, then, another well-known store,
There as before he pitches them his gammon,
He buys some fish, and asks for Bass's ale,
To help wash down the tin of pickled salmon;
The man, completely taken off his guard,
Supplied the bitter without hesitation,
And, having done a jolly morning's work,
The trap goes off and lays an information.

Next morning, the delinquents there are seen
Up at the court, with blank and dismal faces,
And soon the sitting magistrates come in,
And on the bench they take their various places;
They have to fork out fifty pounds of course,
And view the trap with bitter indignation,
Who, on conviction, pockets his five notes,
Besides his pay, for every information.

The Green New Chum

Come all of you assembled here,
Just listen for a while,
I'll give you my adventures now,
At which I know you'll smile.
In the Colony I've just arrived,
My togs, I know, look rum;
And you can see with half an eye
That I'm a green new chum.

I came out here like many more
To pick up lots of gold;
If I greased my boots 'twould stick to them,
At home I had been told;
But deuce a nugget could I find
When up here I had come,
And now I see that I have been
A deluded green new chum.

I went and bought a shovel
And a thundering heavy pick,
The eye of it, I'm confident,
Was full four inches thick.
Two diggers then were passing by,
One pointed with his thumb
And said, 'Lor' Bill, just twig his tools,
There goes a green new chum.' . . .

Two diggers working close by me,
Said they were going to town,
And asked me if I'd buy their hole,
And begged me to go down.
They scraped up nuggets with a knife,
The sight quite struck me dumb;
I gave an ounce-and-a-half for it,
Like a foolish, green new chum.

Next morning I well fossicked it,
And washed the bottom out;
The tub turned out a pennyweight,
And I began to doubt.
Of course you know they'd peppered it,
The gold was all a hum;
They'd sold it me because they saw
I was a green new chum . . .

The Old Whim-Horse

Edward Dyson

He's an old grey horse, with his head bowed sadly,
And with dim old eyes and a queer roll aft,
With the off-fore sprung and the hind screwed badly
And he bears all over the brands of graft;
And he lifts his head from the grass to wonder
Why by night and day now the whim is still,
Why the silence is, and the stampers' thunder
Sounds forth no more from the shattered mill.

In that whim he worked when the night-winds bellowed
On the riven summit of Giant's Hand,
And by day when prodigal Spring had yellowed
All the wide, long sweep of enchanted land;
And he knew his shift, and the whistle's warning,
And he knew the calls of the boys below;
Through the years, unbidden, at night or morning,
He had taken his stand by the old whim bow.

But the whim stands still, and the wheeling swallow
In the silent shaft hangs her home of clay,
And the lizards flirt and the swift snakes follow
O'er the grass-grown brace in the summer day;
And the corn springs high in the cracks and corners
Of the forge, and down where the timber lies;
And the crows are perched like a band of mourners
On the broken hut on the Hermit's Rise.

All the hands have gone, for the rich reef paid out,
And the company waits till the calls come in;
But the old grey horse, like the claim, is played out,
And no market's near for his bones and skin.
So they let him live, and they left him grazing
By the creek, and oft in the evening dim
I have seen him stand on the rises, gazing
At the ruined brace and the rotting whim.

The floods rush high in the gully under,
And the lightnings lash at the shrinking trees,
Or the cattle down from the ranges blunder
As the fires drive by on the summer breeze.
Still the feeble horse at the right hour wanders
To the lonely ring, though the whistle's dumb,
And with hanging head by the bow he ponders
Where the whim-boy's gone — why the shifts don't come.

But there comes a night when he sees lights glowing
In the roofless huts and the ravaged mill,
When he hears again the stampers going
Though the huts are dark and the stampers still:

When he sees the steam to the black roof clinging
As its shadows roll in the silver sands,
And he knows the voice of his driver singing,
And the knocker's clang where the braceman stands.

See the old horse take, like a creature dreaming,
On the ring once more his accustomed place;
But the moonbeams full on the ruins streaming
Show the scattered timbers and grass-grown brace.
Yet he hears the sled in the smithy falling
And the empty truck as it rattles back,
And the boy who stands by the anvil, calling;
And he turns and backs, and he takes up slack.

While the old drum creaks, and the shadows shiver
As the wind sweeps by and the hut doors close,
And the bats dip down in the shaft or quiver
In the ghostly light, round the grey horse goes;
And he feels the strain on his untouched shoulder,
Hears again the voice that was dear to him,
Sees the form he knew — and his heart grows bolder
As he works his shift by the broken whim.

He hears in the sluices the water rushing
As the buckets drain and the doors fall back:
When the early dawn in the east is blushing,
He is limping still round the old, old track.
Now he pricks his ears, with a neigh replying
To a call unspoken, with eyes aglow,
And he sways and sinks in the circle, dying;
From the ring no more will the grey horse go.

In a gully green, where a dam lies gleaming,
And the bush creeps back on a worked-out claim,
And the sleepy crows in the sun sit dreaming
On the timbers grey and a charred hut frame,
Where the legs slant down, and the hare is squatting
In the high rank grass by the dried-up course,
Nigh a shattered drum and a king-post rotting
Are the bleaching bones of the old grey horse.

Cameron's Heart

Henry Lawson

The diggings were just in their glory when Alister Cameron came,
With recommendations, he told me, from friends and a parson
    'at hame',
He read me his recommendations — he called them a part of his
    plant —
The first one was signed by an Elder — the other by Cameron's
    aunt.

The meenister called him 'ungodly — a stray frae the fauld o' the
    Lord',
And his aunt set him down as a spendthrift, 'a rebel at hame and
    abroad'.

He shunned all the girls in the camp, and they said he was proof to
    the dart —
That nothing but whisky and gaming had ever a place in his heart;
He carried a packet about him, well hid, but I saw it at last.
And — well, 'tis a very old story — the story of Cameron's past:
A ring and a sprig o' white heather, a letter or two and a curl,
A bit of worn silver chain, and the portrait of Cameron's girl.

It chanced in the first of the Sixties that Ally and I and McKean
Were sinking a shaft on Mundoorin, near Fosberry's puddle-machine.
The bucket we used was a big one, and rather a weight when 'twas
    full,
Though Alister wound it up easy, for he had the strength of a bull.
He hinted at heart-disease often, but, setting his fancy apart,
I always believed there was nothing the matter with Cameron's
    heart.

One day I was working below — I was filling the bucket with clay,
When Alister cried, 'Pack it on, mon! we ought to be bottomed
    to-day.'
He wound, and the bucket rose steady and swift to the surface until
It reached the first log on the top, where it suddenly stopped, and
    hung still.
I knew what was up in a moment when Cameron shouted to me:
'Climb for you life by the footholes. *I'll stick tae th' haun'le — or dee!'*

And those were the last words he uttered. He groaned, for I heard
    him quite plain —
There's nothing so awful as than when it's wrung from a workman
    in pain.
The strength of despair was upon me; I started, and scarcely drew
    breath,
But climbed to the top for my life in the fear of a terrible death.
And there, with his waist on the handle, I saw the dead form of my
    mate,
And over the shaft hung the bucket, suspended by Cameron's
    weight.

I wonder did Alister think of the scenes in the distance so dim,
When Death at the windlass that morning took cruel advantage of
    him?
He knew if the bucket rushed down it would murder or cripple his
    mate —
His hand on the iron was closed with a grip that was stronger than
    Fate;
He thought of my danger, not his, when he felt in his bosom the
    smart,
And stuck to the handle in spite of the Finger of Death on his heart.

Look Out Below!

A young man left his native shores,
For trade was bad at home;
To seek his fortune in this land
He crossed the briny foam;
And when he came to Ballarat,
It put him in a glow,
To hear the sound of the windlass,
And the cry 'Look out below!'

Wherever he turned his wandering eyes
Great wealth he did behold —
And peace and plenty hand in hand,
By the magic power of gold;
Quoth he, 'As I am young and strong,
To the diggings I will go;
For I like the sound of the windlass,
And the cry "Look out below!" '

Amongst the rest he took his chance,
And his luck at first was vile;
But he still resolved to persevere,
And at length he made his pile.
So says he, 'I'll take my passage,
And home again I'll go,
And I'll say farewell to the windlass,
And the cry "Look out below!" '

Arrived in London once again,
His gold he freely spent,
And into every gaiety
And dissipation went.
But pleasure, if prolonged too much,
Oft causes pain, you know;
And he missed the sound of the windlass,
And the cry 'Look out below!'

And thus he reasoned with himself —
'Oh, why did I return,
For the digger's independent life
I now begin to yearn.
Here purse-proud lords the poor oppress,
But there it is not so;
Give me the sound of the windlass,
And the cry "Look out below!" '

Bush Life

Bush Life

The ballads in this section cover much of the period of Australia's settlement by Europeans. Explorer Ernest Favenc's 'The Watchers' records some of the horrors awaiting the first white explorers and settlers to venture into the harsh country of the inland.

Squatters followed the explorers and took up the land, dispossessing the Aboriginal people whose desperate but doomed defence of their land against the better-equipped settlers is described in part in Charles Harpur's famous 'The Creek of the Four Graves'. But life for the squatters was not always easy. Gordon's 'Exodus Parthenidae' and Lawson's 'Middleton's Rouseabout' both describe the failure and defeat of squatting families driven off the land by bad seasons, bushfires and debts.

The next trial for the surviving squatters was the advent of small selectors and farmers who often took up some of the squatters' best land, cutting off access to water, and fencing and farming the land the squatter had used for grazing cattle and sheep. Lawson describes a typically bitter battle between squatter and selector in 'The Fire at Ross's Farm', and 'The Eumerella Shore' is a cheeky selectors' song sung at the expense of the squatter.

It must have been a lonely life, especially for the women, who were not as free simply to move on as the men were. Some of the sorrows and frustrations of such a life are captured in Lawson's 'The Bush Girl', but for a less sentimental view of women's life in the bush, none can surpass the short stories of Barbara Baynton.

Isolation and vast distances made transport especially important. Goods and produce were usually hauled across country by bullock drays driven by foul-mouthed old bushmen, while Cobb and Co coaches carried people and goods in slightly more comfort. Henry Lawson was one of many Australians who remembered the coaches with nostalgia, and, while fewer people may have treasured particularly tender memories of the rough old bullockies, two of their many songs are included in this chapter.

Now sealed highways circle the continent, and communication networks, efficient transport, and the flying doctor service have almost overcome the dangers and isolation of bush life, but these songs and ballads still remind us of how dearly some of these comforts have been won.

A Wildflower by the Way

Will H. Ogilvie

The sun-rays burned like brands a-fire,
And, with a half-mile spread,
In blue grass to their heart's desire
The big Windorahs fed.

I rode the wing — a frail pretence;
What trick doth Love disdain? —
And halted at the split-rail fence
And fastened Gauntlet's rein.

She stood before her cottage home,
A maid of dimpled charms,
And churned the suds to snow-white foam
Across her nut-brown arms.

Then flashed those splendid orbs of brown:
She whispered soft and low,
'I'd love to see this Sydney town
Where all the cattle go!'

I took her sun-kissed hand and said
(And half believed it true);
'No lady there has lips so red
Or arms so soft as you —

'Or eyes one-half so bright!' I chaffed
To pass dull time away;
But Brown Eyes of the Barwon laughed,
'So all you drovers say!'

I had no longer need to speak —
Chained by those eyes of brown,
I kissed her once for Barwon Creek
And twice for Sydney town;

Then gathered bridle-rein once more
And heard a heart-beat say,
'The drover's life were dull but for
The wildflowers by the way!'

The Bush Girl

Henry Lawson

So you rode from the range where your brothers 'select'
Through the ghostly grey bush in the dawn —
You rode slowly at first, lest her heart should suspect
That you were so glad to be gone;
You had scarcely the courage to glance back at her
By the homestead receding from view,
And you breathed with relief as you rounded the spur,
For the world was a wide world to you.

Grey eyes that grow sadder than sunset or rain,
Fond heart that is ever more true,
Firm faith that grows firmer for watching in vain —
She'll wait by the sliprails for you.

Ah! the world is a new and wide one to you,
But the world to your sweetheart is shut,
For a change never comes to the lonely Bush girl
From the stockyard, the bush, and the hut;

And the only relief from its dullness she feels
Is when ridges grow softened and dim,
And away in the dusk to the sliprails she steals
To dream of past meetings 'with him'.

Do you think, where, in place of bare fences, dry creeks,
Clear streams and green hedges are seen —
Where the girls have the lily and rose in their cheeks,
And the grass in midsummer is green —
Do you think now and then, now or then, in the whirl
Of the city, while London is new,
Of the hut in the Bush, and the freckled-faced girl
Who is eating her heart out for you?

Grey eyes that are sadder than sunset or rain,
Bruised heart that is ever more true,
Fond faith that is firmer for trusting in vain —
She waits by the sliprails for you.

The Fire at Ross's Farm

Henry Lawson

The squatter saw his pastures wide
Decrease, as one by one
The farmers moving to the west
Selected on his run;
Selectors took the water up
And all the black soil round;
The best grass-land the squatter had
Was spoilt by Ross's Ground.

Now many schemes to shift old Ross
Had racked the squatter's brains,
But Sandy had the stubborn blood
Of Scotland in his veins;
He held the land and fenced it in,
He cleared and ploughed the soil,
And year by year a richer crop
Repaid him for his toil.

Between the homes for many years
The devil left his tracks;
The squatter pounded Ross's stock,
And Sandy pounded Black's.
A well upon the lower run
Was filled with earth and logs,
And Black laid baits about the farm
To poison Ross's dogs.

It was, indeed, a deadly feud
Of class and creed and race,
But, yet, there was a Romeo
And a Juliet in the case;
And more than once across the flats,
Beneath the Southern Cross,
Young Robert Black was seen to ride
With pretty Jenny Ross.

One Christmas time, when months of drought
Had parched the western creeks,
The bushfires started in the north
And travelled south for weeks.
At night along the river-side
The scene was grand and strange —
The hill-fires looked like lighted streets
Of cities in the range.

The cattle-tracks between the trees
Were like long dusky aisles,
And on a sudden breeze the fire
Would sweep along for miles;

Like sounds of distant musketry
It crackled through the brakes,
And o'er the flat of silver grass
It hissed like angry snakes.

It leapt across the flowing streams
And raced the pastures broad;
It climbed the trees, and lit the boughs,
And through the scrubs it roared.
The bees fell stifled in the smoke
Or perished in their hives,
And with the stock the kangaroos
Went flying for their lives.

The sun had set on Christmas Eve,
When, through the scrub-lands wide
Young Robert Black came riding home
As only natives ride.
He galloped to the homestead door
And gave the first alarm:
'The fire is past the granite spur,
And close to Ross's farm.

'Now, father, send the men at once,
They won't be wanted here;
Poor Ross's wheat is all he has
To pull him through the year.'
'Then let it burn,' the squatter said;
'I'd like to see it done —
I'd bless the fire if it would clear
Selectors from the run.

'Go, if you will,' the squatter said,
'You shall not take the men —
Go out and join your precious friends,
And don't come back again.'
'I won't come back,' young Robert cried,
And, reckless in his ire,
He sharply turned his horse's head
And galloped towards the fire.

And there for three long weary hours,
Half-blinded with smoke and heat,
Old Ross and Robert fought the flames
That neared the ripened wheat.
The farmer's hand was nerved by fears
Of danger and of loss;
And Robert fought the stubborn foe
For the love of Jenny Ross.

But serpent-like the curves and lines
Slipped past them and between,
Until they reached the bound'ry where

The old coach-road had been.
'The track is now our only hope,
There we must stand,' cried Ross,
'For nought on earth can stop the fire
If once it gets across.'

Then came a cruel gust of wind,
And, with a fiendish rush,
The flames leapt o'er the narrow path
And lit the fence of brush.
'The crop must burn!' the farmer cried,
'We cannot save it now,'
And down upon the blackened ground
He dashed the ragged bough.

But wildly, in a rush of hope,
His heart began to beat,
For o'er the crackling fire he heard
The sound of horses' feet.
'Here's help at last,' young Robert cried,
And even as he spoke
The squatter with a dozen men
Came racing through the smoke.

Down on the ground the stockmen jumped
And bared each brawny arm;
They tore green branches from the trees
And fought for Ross's farm;
And when before the gallant band
The beaten flames gave way,
Two grimy hands in friendship joined —
And it was Christmas Day.

Wallaby Stew

Poor Dad he got a five year stretch as everybody knows,
And now he lives in Boggo Road with broad arrows on his clothes.
He branded old Brown's cleanskins, and never left a tail;
So I'll relate the family's fate since Father went to jail.

So, stir the wallaby stew! Make soup of the kangaroo tail!
I tell you things is pretty crook since Father went to jail.

Our sheep all died a month ago, not rot but blooming fluke;
The cow was boozed last Christmas Day by elder brother Luke;
I sold the buggy on my own, the place is up for sale,
That won't be all that has been junked when Dad gets out of jail!

Our Bess got shook upon some bloke who's gone we don't know
    where;
He used to act around the sheds, but he ain't acted square.
And Mother's got a shearer-cove forever on her tail —
The family will have grown a bit when Dad gets out of jail!

They let Dad out before his time to give us a surprise.
He looked around at all of us and gently blessed our eyes;
He shook hands with the shearer-cove, and said that things
    seemed stale
Then left him there to shepherd us, and battled back to jail.

Exodus Parthenidae

THE LAY OF THE LAST SQUATTER
Adam Lindsay Gordon

Draw your chair to the fire, old woman,
The days are warm, but the nights are cold;
So, they've hunted our milkers off the common,
And pounded them, calves and all, I'm told.
Had I caught 'Long Henderson' driving 'Molly',
I'd have made him tell me 'the reason why',
He'd scarcely have answered you so jolly,
Had I turned the corner suddenly.

Faith, 'tis time we laid our oars in the rullocks,
We've got no right of commonage now,
And the sheep are sold, and the working bullocks
And the cattle, all but the strawberry cow;
I felt my heart for the moment soften
When the butcher offered me three pound five
For the poor old thing that you've milked so often -
She sha'n't be slaughtered while I'm alive.

And Robinson Brown has sent me his bill, dear,
And Morton Jones has taken the lease,
And the kangaroo dogs, 'Lion' and 'Kildeer',
Are sold for fifty shillings apiece;
I'm sorry to part with the red dog, truly,
At fifty shillings I call him cheap,
But the brindled dog is a trifle unruly —
Oh! Carrington Jackson, mind your sheep.

I'm sure if Giles is satisfied, I am;
The horses averaged well, and though
I'd like to have kept the colt by 'Priam',
'Tis just as well that I let him go;
For if my creditors won't be losers,
I've set them scratching their heads, mayhap,
And you know that some folk mustn't be choosers,
Which folk I belong to — 'verbum sap'.

I've had an interview with the banker,
And I found him civil, and even kind;
But the game's up here, we must weigh the anchor,
We've the surf before, and the rocks behind;
So trim the canvas, and clear the gangways,
They've got the great unwashed on their side;
It's no use sparring with 'Templar Strangways',
It's no use kicking at 'Lavender Glyde'.

And I guess it's all U P with the squatter;
The people are crying aloud for the land;

They've made it hot, and they'll find it hotter
When they plough the limestone and sow the sand.
'All flesh is grass,' so saith the preacher;
'All grass is ours,' quoth Randolph Stow;
Is the man related to Harriet Beecher?
With *mobile vulgus* he's all the go.

And, years to come, in the book of Hansard,
You may read the tale of the frogs retold,
How they prayed for a king, how their prayer was answered,
How the king was crowned, and the frogs were sold,
How they ended, the schemes whose names were 'Legion',
In the Mephistopheles laughter note,
From the depths of 'the Mariner's' gastric region,
That rattled up to his innocent throat.

I wish you'd write me a line to Maddox
(My fingers are cramped with that boring brute);
I'll take his bid for the purchased paddocks,
The sum we mentioned he won't dispute.
I might have made better terms with Parker
If he hadn't known I was forced to sell,
But I couldn't have kept these matters darker,
I didn't try to — 'tis just as well.

Fred Carson made an offer for Lancer —
'Twas a little less than his hide would bring;
You may guess I gave him a civil answer,
Which put a stop to his huckstering;
I loosed the old nag at the sliding railing,
And carried my saddle up to the hut;
His eyes, as well as his limbs, are failing,
He scarcely knew when the gate was shut.

Aye, troubles are coming upon us thickly,
'Tis hard to leave the old place at last,
And you're not strong, and the baby's sickly,
And your mother's ailing and aging fast.
I remember the days when credit was plenty,
And years were few; but those days are o'er;
Old Beranger sings of the joys of twenty,
But I shall never see thirty more.

It's no use talking, things might be better,
And then again they might well be worse —
You needn't trouble about that letter,
The youngster's squalling loud for a nurse;
And your hand is surely rather unsteady,
That writing looks to be all askew,
What! are there tears in your eyes already?
Come, old girl, this will never do!

* * *

I might have taken Time by the forelock,
I might have made my hay in the sun,
I might have foreseen — but wizard or warlock
Could never undo what once is done.
And at least I've wantonly injured no man,
Although I've lived on the people's land —
Draw your chair to the fire, old woman,
And mix a drop of the battle-axe brand.

Scots of the Riverina

Henry Lawson

The boy ran away to the city from his home at Christmas time —
They were Scots of the Riverina, and to run from home was a crime.
The old man burned his letter, the first and last he burned,
And he scratched his name from the Bible when the old woman's
    back was turned.

A year went past, and another; and the fruit went down the line.
They heard the boy had enlisted, but the old man made no sign.
His name must never be mentioned on the farm by Gundagai —
They were Scots of the Riverina with ever the kirk hard by.

The boy came home on his 'final', and the township's bonfire burned.
His mother's arms were about him, but the old man's back was
    turned.
The daughters begged for pardon till the old man raised his hand —
A Scot of the Riverina who was hard to understand.

The boy was killed in Flanders, where the bravest heroes die.
There were tears at the Grahame homestead, and grief in Gundagai;
But the old man ploughed at daybreak and the old man ploughed till
    the mirk —
There were furrows of pain in the orchard while his housefolk went
    to the kirk.

The hurricane-lamp in the rafters dimly and dimly burned,
And the old man died at the table when the old woman's back was
    turned.
Face down on his bare arms folded he sank with his wild grey hair
Outspread o'er the open Bible and a name re-written there.

Middleton's Rouseabout

Henry Lawson

Tall and freckled and sandy,
Face of a country lout;
This was the picture of Andy,
Middleton's Rouseabout.

Type of a coming nation
In the land of cattle and sheep;
Worked on Middleton's station,
Pound a week and his keep;

On Middleton's wide dominions
Plied the stockwhip and shears;
Hadn't any opinions,
Hadn't any 'idears'.

Swiftly the years went over,
Liquor and drought prevailed;
Middleton went as a drover
After his station had failed.

Type of a careless nation,
Men who are soon played out,
Middleton was: — and his station
Was bought by the Rouseabout.

Flourishing beard and sandy,
Tall and solid and stout;
This is the picture of Andy,
Middleton's Rouseabout.

Now on his own dominions
Works with his overseers;
Hasn't any opinions,
Hasn't any idears.

The Creek of the Four Graves

Charles Harpur

I

A settler in the olden times went forth
With four of his most bold and trusted men
Into the wilderness — went forth to seek
New streams and wider pastures for his fast
Increasing flocks and herds. O'er mountain routes
And over wild wolds clouded up with brush,
And cut with marshes perilously deep, —
So went they forth at dawn; at eve the sun,
That rose behind them as they journeyed out,
Was firing with his nether rim a range
Of unknown mountains, that like ramparts towered
Full in their front; . . .

Before them thus extended, wilder grew
The scene each moment and more beautiful;
For when the sun was all but sunk below
Those barrier mountains, in the breeze that o'er
Their rough enormous backs deep-fleeced with wood
Came whispering down, the wide up-slanting sea
Of fanning leaves in the descending rays
Danced dazzlingly, tingling as if the trees
Thrilled to the roots for very happiness. . .

Here halting wearied now the sun was set,
Our travellers kindled for their first night's camp
A brisk and crackling fire, which seemed to them
A wilder creature than 'twas elsewhere wont,
Because of the surrounding savageness. . .

At last, the business of the supper done,
The echoes of the solitary place
Came as in sylvan wonder wide about
To hear and imitate the voices strange,
Within the pleasant purlieus of the fire
Lifted in glee; but to be hushed erelong,
As with the darkness of the night there came
O'er the adventurers, each and all, some sense
Of danger lurking in its forest lairs.

But, nerved by habit, they all gathered round
About the well built fire, whose nimble tongues
Sent up continually a strenuous roar
Of fierce delight, and from their fuming pipes
Drawing rude comfort, round the pleasant light
With grave discourse they planned their next day's deeds.
Wearied at length, their couches they prepared
Of rushes, and the long green tresses pulled
From the bent boughs of the wild willows near;
Then the four men stretched out their tired limbs
Under the dark arms of the forest trees
That mixed aloft, high in the starry air,
In arcs and leafy domes whose crossing curves,
Blended with denser intergrowth of sprays,
Were seen in mass traced out against the clear
Wide gaze of heaven; and trustful of the watch
Kept near them by their master, soon they slept,
Forgetful of the perilous wilderness
That lay around them like a spectral world;
And all things slept; . . .

II

His lone watch
The master kept, and wakeful looked abroad
On all the solemn beauty of the world;
And by some sweet and subtle tie that joins
The loved and cherished, absent from our side,
With all that is serene and beautiful
In Nature, thoughts of home began to steal
Into his musings — when, on a sudden, hark!
A bough cracks loudly in a neighbouring brake!
Against the shade-side of a bending gum.
With a strange horror gathering to his heart,
As if his blood were charged with insect life
And writhed along in clots, he stilled himself
And listened heedfully, till his held breath
Became a pang. Nought heard he: silence there
Had recomposed her ruffled wings, and now
Deep brooded in the darkness; so that he
Again mused on, quiet and reassured.

But there again — crack upon crack! Awake!
O heaven! have hell's worst fiends burst howling up
Into the death-doomed world? Or whence, if not
From diabolic rage, could surge a yell
So horrible as that which now affrights
The shuddering dark! Beings as fell are near!
Yea, beings in their dread inherited hate
Awful, vengeful as hell's worst fiends, are come
In vengeance! For behold from the long grass
And nearer brakes arise the bounding forms
Of painted savages, full in the light
Thrown outward by the fire, that roused and lapped
The rounding darkness with its ruddy tongues
More fiercely than before, as though even it
Had felt the sudden shock the air received
From those terrific cries.

On then they came
And rushed upon the sleepers, three of whom

But started, and then weltered prone beneath
The first fell blow dealt down on each by three
Of the most stalwart of their pitiless foes;
But one again, and yet again, rose up,
Rose to his knees, under the crushing strokes
Of huge clubbed nulla-nullas, till his own
Warm blood was blinding him. For he was one
Who had with misery nearly all his days
Lived lonely, and who therefore in his soul
Did hunger after hope, and thirst for what
Hope still had promised him, some taste at least
Of human good however long deferred;
And now he could not, even in dying, loose
His hold on life's poor chances still to come,
Could not but so dispute the terrible fact
Of death, e'en in death's presence. Strange it is,
Yet oft 'tis seen, that fortune's pampered child
Consents to death's untimely power with less
Reluctance, less despair, than does the wretch
Who hath been ever blown about the world,
The straw-like sport of fate's most bitter blasts;
So though the shadows of untimely death,
Inevitably under every stroke
But thickened more and more, against them still
The poor wretch struggled, nor would cease until
One last great blow, dealt down upon his head
As if in mercy, gave him to the dust,
With all his many woes and frustrate hopes.

The master, chilled with horror, saw it all;
From instinct more than conscious thought he raised
His death-charged tube, and at that murderous crew
Firing, saw one fall ox-like to the earth,
Then turned and fled. Fast fled he, but as fast
His deadly foes went thronging on his track.
Fast! for in full pursuit behind him yelled
Men whose wild speech no work for mercy hath!
And as he fled the forest beasts as well
In general terror through the brakes ahead
Crashed scattering, or with maddening speed athwart
His course came frequent. On, still on, he flies —
Flies for dear life, and still behind him hears
Nearer and nearer, the light rapid dig
Of many feet — nearer and nearer still.

III

So went the chase. Now at a sudden turn
Before him lay the steep-banked mountain creek;
Still on he kept perforce, and from a rock
That beaked the bank, a promontory bare,
Plunging right forth and shooting feet-first down,

Sunk to his middle in the flashing stream,
In which the imaged stars seemed all at once
To burst like rockets into one wide blaze.
Then wading through the ruffled waters, forth
He sprang, and seized a snake-like root that from
The opponent bank protruded, clenching there
His cold hand like a clamp of steel; and thence
He swung his dripping form aloft, the blind
And breathless haste of one who flies for life
Urging him on; up the dark ledge he climbed, . . .

There in its face a cavity he felt,
The upper earth of which in one rude mass
Was held fast bound by the enwoven roots
Of two old trees, and which, beneath the mould,
Over the dark and clammy cave below,
Twisted like knotted snakes. 'Neath these he crept,
Just as the dark forms of his hunters thronged
The steep bold rock whence he before had plunged. . .

Keen was their search but vain,
There grouped in dark knots standing in the stream
That glimmered past them moaning as it went,
They marvelled; passing strange to them it seemed;
Some old mysterious fable of their race,
That brooded o'er the valley and the creek,
Returned upon their minds, and fear-struck all
And silent, they withdrew. And when the sound
Of their retreating steps had died away,
As back they hurried to despoil the dead
In the stormed camp, then rose the fugitive,
Renewed his flight, nor rested from it, till
He gained the shelter of his longed-for home.
And in that glade, far in the doomful wild,
In sorrowing record of an awful hour
Of human agony and loss extreme,
Untimely spousals with a desert death,
Four grassy mounds are there beside the creek,
Bestrewn with sprays and leaves from the old trees
Which moan the ancient dirges that have caught
The heed of dying ages, and for long
The traveller passing then in safety there
Would call the place — The Creek of the Four Graves.

The Watchers

Ernest Favenc

All things were old in that grim grey land,
All things were withered and sere:
There was no one left, save a grisly band
Who fought for their lives with a slackened hand,
For life had ceased to be dear.

Under the curse of a pitiless sun
And the drought of rainless years
They had fallen and slumbered one by one,
Thankful alone that their task was done —
There was no more toil or tears.

'Neath a stunted tree on the rocky crest
Of a ridge of barren stone
They gazed on the arid plain to west
And sighed as they turned from their hopeless quest
And the three stood there alone —

Alone, save for an unseen two,
Who watched the others there:
Gaunt as the desert land to view,
Unwatered by rain, unslaked by dew
They sat there, a ghastly pair.

For one was old, who had never been born,
Although mortal look he bore:
His wings were draggled, his pinions torn,
He carried a scythe that was notched and worn;
And he turned an hour-glass o'er.

But the other had a more ghastly form,
That no man could live and see:
His fleshless bones had never been warm:
He lived in carnage, disease and storm,
And a constant grin wore he.

'Old comrade mine,' quoth Time at last,
'How long shall they make their moan?'
Croaked Death, 'When the sands have slowly passed
Thrice through thy hour-glass, my dart I'll cast,'
And he sharpened it on a stone.

Time scooped up a handful of heated sand:
'I love this well,' cried he.
'When my glass needs filling I seek this land' —
And he poured it out of his wasted hand —
'Oh! the desert sand for me'.

Afar in the east a cloud appeared
With the thunder's muttered sound;
Darker it grew as the group it neared.
'Twould come too late, the doomed men feared;
Time turned his hour-glass round.

And ever they watched it as it spread.
And dreamt of the welcome rain,
While the air grew chill 'neath the Storm-sprite's tread
And the sky was murk with a hue of lead —
Time turned his glass again.

Death chuckled and held his dart up first,
Time turned his hour-glass round;
The storm-clouds eddied, and raged, and burst,
But never could slake a dead man's thirst —
Three dead men lay on the ground.

Knocking Around

Henry Lawson

Weary old wife, with the bucket and cow,
'How's your son Jack? and where is he now?'
Haggard old eyes that turn to the west —
'Boys will be boys, and he's gone with the rest!'
Grief without tears and grief without sound;
'Somewhere up-country he's knocking around.'
  Knocking around with a vagabond crew,
  Does for himself what a mother would do;
  Maybe in trouble and maybe hard-up,
  Maybe in want of a bite or a sup;
  Dead of the fever, or lost in the drought,
  Lonely old mother! he's knocking about.

Wiry old man at the tail of the plough,
'Heard of Jack lately? and where is he now?'
Pauses a moment his forehead to wipe,
Drops the rope reins while he feels for his pipe,
Scratches his grey head in sorrow or doubt:
'Somewhere or other he's knocking about.'
  Knocking about on the runs of the West,
  Holding his own with the worst and the best,
  Breaking in horses and risking his neck,
  Droving or shearing and making a cheque;
  Straight as a sapling — six-foot, and sound,
  Jack is all right when he's knocking around.

The Old Bullock Dray

Oh! the shearing is all over, and the wool is coming down,
And I mean to get a wife, boys, when I go down to town,
Everything that's got two legs presents itself to view,
From the little paddy-melon to the bucking kangaroo.

'So it's roll up your blankets, and let's make a push,
I'll take you up the country and show you the bush.
I'll be bound you won't get such a chance another day,
So come and take possession of my old Bullock-dray.

Now, I've saved up a good cheque and I mean to buy a team,
And when I get a wife, boys, I'll be all-serene;
For, calling at the depot, they say there's no delay
To get an off-sider for the old Bullock-dray.

I'll teach you the whip, and the bullocks how to flog,
You'll be my off-sider when we're stuck in a bog:
Lashing out both left and right and every other way,
Making skin, hair and blood fly round the old Bullock-dray.

Oh! we'll live like fighting-cocks, for good living I'm your man,
We'll have leather-jacks, johnny-cakes, and fritters in the pan;
Or if you want some fish, why, I'll catch you some soon;
For we'll bob for barramundies round the banks of a lagoon.

Oh! yes, of beef and damper I make sure we have enough,
And we'll boil in the bucket such a whopper of a duff:
And our friends will dance to the honour of the day,
To the music of the bells, around the old Bullock-dray.

Oh! we'll have plenty girls, we must mind that.
There'll be 'Buck-jumping Maggie' and 'Leather-belly Pat.'
There'll be 'Stringybark Peggy' and 'Green-Hide Mike'.
Yes, my Colonials, just as many as you like!

The Eumeralla Shore

There's a happy little valley on the Eumeralla shore,
Where I've lingered many happy hours away,
On my little free selection I have acres by the score,
Where I unyoke the bullocks from the dray.

To my bullocks then I say, no matter where you stray,
You will never be impounded any more;
For you're running, running, running on the duffer's piece of land,
Free selected on the Eumeralla shore.

When the moon has climbed the mountains and stars are
     shining bright,
Then we saddle up our horses and away,

And we steal the squatters' cattle in the darkness of the night,
And we brand 'em at the dawning of the day.

Oh, my little poddy calf, at the squatter you may laugh,
For he'll never be your owner any more;
For you're running, running, running on the duffer's piece of land
Free selected on the Eumeralla shore.

The Free-selector's Daughter

Henry Lawson

I met her on the Lachlan Side —
A darling girl I thought her,
And ere I left I swore I'd win
The free-selector's daughter.

I milked her father's cows a month,
I brought the wood and water,
I mended all the broken fence,
Before I won the daughter.

I listened to her father's yarns,
I did just what I 'oughter',
And what you'll have to do to win
A free-selector's daughter.

I broke my pipe and burnt my twist,
And washed my mouth with water;
I had a shave before I kissed
The free-selector's daughter.

Then, rising in the frosty morn,
I brought the cows for Mary,
And when I'd milked a bucketful
I took it to the dairy.

I poured the milk into the dish
While Mary held the strainer,
I summoned heart to speak my wish,
And, oh! her blush grew plainer.

I told her I must leave the place,
I said that I would miss her;
At first she turned away her face,
And then she let me kiss her.

I put the bucket on the ground,
And in my arms I caught her;
I'd give the world to hold again
That free selector's daughter.

The Lights of Cobb and Co

Henry Lawson

Fire lighted, on the table a meal for sleepy men,
A lantern in the stable, a jingle now and then;
The mail coach looming darkly by light of moon and star,
The growl of sleepy voices — a candle in the bar;
A stumble in the passage of folk with wits abroad;
A swear-word from a bedroom — the shout of 'All aboard!'
'Tchk-tchk! Git-up!' 'Hold fast, there!' and down the range we go;
Five hundred miles of scattered camps will watch for Cobb and Co.

Old coaching towns already 'decaying for their sins',
Uncounted 'Half-Way Houses', and scores of 'Ten Mile Inns';
The riders from the stations by lonely granite peaks;
The black-boy for the shepherds on sheep and cattle creeks;
The roaring camps of Gulgong, and many a 'Digger's Rest';
The diggers on the Lachlan; the huts of Furthest West;
Some twenty thousand exiles who sailed for weal or woe;
The bravest hearts of twenty lands will wait for Cobb and Co.

The morning star has vanished, the frost and fog are gone,
In one of those grand mornings which but on mountains dawn;
A flask of friendly whisky — each other's hopes we share —
And throw our top-coats open to drink the mountain air.
The roads are rare to travel, and life seems all complete;
The grind of wheels on gravel, the trot of horses' feet,
The trot, trot, trot, and canter, as down the spur we go —
The green sweeps to horizons blue that call for Cobb and Co.

We take a bright girl actress through western dust and damps,
To bear the home-world message, and sing for sinful camps,
To wake the hearts and break them, wild hearts that hope
    and ache —
(Ah! when she thinks of *those* days her own must nearly break!)
Five miles this side the gold-field, a loud, triumphant shout:
Five hundred cheering diggers have snatched the horses out:
With 'Auld Lang Syne' in chorus through roaring camps they go —
That cheer for her, and cheer for Home, and cheer for Cobb and Co.

Three lamps above the rides and gorges dark and deep,
A flash on sandstone cuttings where sheer the sidings sweep,
A flash on shrouded wagons, on water ghastly white;
Weird bush and scattered remnants of 'rushes in the night';
Across the swollen river a flash beyond the ford:
'Ride hard to warn the driver! He's drunk or mad, good Lord!'
But on the bank to westward a broad, triumphant glow —
A hundred miles shall see tonight the lights of Cobb and Co!

Swift scramble up the siding where teams climb inch by inch;
Pause, bird-like, on the summit — then breakneck down the pinch
Past haunted half-way houses — where convicts made the bricks —

Scrub-yards and new bark shanties, we dash with five and six —
By clear, ridge-country rivers, and gaps where tracks run high,
Where waits the lonely horseman, cut clear against the sky;
Through stringy-bark and blue-gum, and box and pine we go;
New camps are stretching 'cross the plains the routes of
    Cobb and Co.

Throw down the reins, old driver — there's no one left to shout;
The ruined inn's survivor must take the horses out.
A poor old coach hereafter! — we're lost to all such things —
No bursts of songs or laughter shall shake your leathern springs
When creeping in unnoticed by railway sidings drear,
Or left in yards for lumber, decaying with the year —
Oh, who'll think how in those days when distant fields were broad
You raced across the Lachlan side with twenty-five on board.

Not all the ships that sail away since Roaring Days are done —
Not all the boats that steam from port, nor all the trains that run,
Shall take such hopes and loyal hearts — for men shall never know
Such days as when the Royal Mail was run by Cobb and Co.
The 'greyhounds' race across the sea, the 'special' cleaves the haze,
But these seem dull and slow to me compared with Roaring Days!
The eyes that watched are dim with age, and souls are weak and
    slow,
The hearts are dust or hardened now that broke for Cobb and Co.

Bullocky Bill

As I came down Talbingo Hill
I heard a maiden cry,
'There's goes old Bill the Bullocky —
He's bound for Gundagai.'

A better poor old beggar
Never cracked an honest crust,
A tougher poor old beggar
Never drug a whip through dust.

His team got bogged on the Five-mile Creek,
Bill lashed and swore and cried,
'If Nobbie don't get me out of this
I'll tattoo his bloody hide.'

But Nobbie strained and broke the yoke
And poked out the leader's eye,
And the dog sat on the tucker-box
Five miles from Gundagai.

The Bush Fire

Henry Lawson

On the runs to the west of the Dingo Scrub there was drought, and
    ruin, and death,
And the sandstorm came from the dread north-east with the blast of
    a furnace-breath;
Till at last one day, at the fierce sunrise, a boundary-rider woke,
And saw in the place of the distant haze a curtain of light-blue
    smoke.

There is saddling-up by the cocky's hut, and out in the station yard,
And away to the north, north-east, north-west, the bushmen are
    riding hard.
The pickets are out, and many a scout, and many a mulga wire,
While Bill and Jim, their faces grim, are riding to meet the fire.

It roars for days in the trackless scrub, and across, where the ground
    seems clear,
With a crackle and rush, like the hissing of snakes, the fire draws
    near and near;
Till at last, exhausted by sleeplessness, and the terrible toil and heat,
The squatter is crying, 'My God! the wool' and the farmer, 'My God!
    the wheat!'

But there comes a drunkard (who reels as he rides) with news from
    the roadside pub; —
'Pat Murphy — the cocky — cut off by the fire! — way back in the
    Dingo Scrub!
Let the wheat and the woolshed go to —' Well, they do as each great
    heart bids;
They are riding a race for the Dingo Scrub — for Pat and his wife
    and his kids.

And who are leading the race with Death? All ill-matched three,
    you'll allow;
Flash Jim, the Breaker, and Boozing Bill (who is riding steadily now),
And Constable Dunn, of the Mounted Police, on the grey between
    the two
(He wants Flash Jim, but that job can wait till they get the Murphys
    through).

As they strike the track through the blazing scrub, the trooper is
    heard to shout;
'We'll take them on to the Two-mile Tank, if we cannot bring them
    out!'
A half-mile more, and the rest rein back, retreating, half-choked, half-
    blind;
And the three are gone from the sight of men, and the bush fire roars
    behind.

The Bushmen wiped the smoke-made tears, and like Bushmen
    laughed and swore

'Poor Bill will be wanting his drink tonight as never he did before.'
'And Dunn was the best in the whole damned force!' says a client of
    Dunn's, with pride;
'I reckon he'll serve his summons on Jim — when they get to the
    other side.'

* * *

It is daylight again, and the fire is past, and the black scrub silent
    and grim
Except for the blaze in an old dead tree, or the crash of a falling limb;
And the Bushmen are riding across the waste, with hearts and with
    eyes that fill,
To look at the bodies of Constable Dunn, Flash Jim, and Boozing Bill.

They are found in the mud of the Two-mile Tank, where a fiend
    might scarce survive,
But the Bushmen gather from words they hear that the bodies are
    much alive.
There is Swearing Pat, with his grey beard singed, and language of
    lurid hue,
And his tough old wife, and his half-baked kids, and the three who
    dragged them through.

Old Pat is deploring his burnt-out home, and his wife the climate
    warm;
And Jim the loss of his favourite horse and Dunn of his uniform;
And Boozing Bill, with a raging thirst, is cursing the Dingo Scrub,
But all he'll ask is the loan of a flask and a lift to the nearest pub.

* * *

Flash Jim the Breaker is lying low — blue-paper is after Jim,
But Dunn, the trooper, is riding his rounds with a blind eye out for
    him;
And Boozing Bill is fighting DTs in the township of Sudden Jerk —
When they're wanted again in the Dingo Scrub, they'll be there to do
    the work.

Bushrangers

Bushrangers

Many Autralians pride themselves on their larrikin streak, which might explain the popularity of some of our bushrangers. Ned Kelly has become a national hero, remembered for his courage and contempt for authority. Some of his contemporaries were appalled by the murders and apparent callousness of the Kelly Gang. 'Stringybark Creek' gives a fairly accurate picture of some of those murders.

Ben Hall, who never murdered anyone, has a stronger claim on our sympathies. He was arrested by Sir Frederick Pottinger of the New South Wales police on trumped-up charges of keeping bushranger Frank Gardiner in supplies, and though acquitted both times, when he returned to his property he found that his wife had left with their son, and all his stock were either dead or missing. Hounded and embittered, Ben Hall turned to bushranging, and took over as the leader of Frank Gardiner's gang after Frank retired to Queensland with a good share of the takings from the Great Gold Escort Robbery in 1862. As 'The Ballad of Ben Hall' recounts, Hall, with his right-hand man John Gilbert, and the gang, did what they pleased for three years, and even captured a town. Ben Hall's most bitter enemies had to admire his courage and character, but in the end, while camped alone one night, he was surrounded by troopers and shot. However, when the Ballad was written, that was all still in the future.

Hall's predecessor, Frank Gardiner, started his career as a horse thief on the Victorian goldfields, and was already a ticket-of-leave man when he began holding up people on the roads around Lambing Flat and 'working' round Carcoar. He not only headed his own gang, but trained many bushrangers, and some young men, wanting to join the gang, committed daring crimes in an effort to impress him. The gang's audacious raids were finally crowned by the Great Gold Escort Robbery at Eugowra Rocks in 1862,

whereupon Gardiner retired to Queensland with his share of the £12 000 and his lover, Mrs Brown (who did not, as the song claims, betray him). Two years later, Detective McGlone finally caught up with him, and he was sentenced to 32 years. After serving 10 as a model prisoner he was pardoned on condition that he leave the country. John Gilbert, who had been both Hall's and Gardiner's right-hand man, was shot by troopers less than a week after Hall while he was still in his twenties. John Dunn was caught and hanged when he was only 22.

'The Wild Colonial Boy', one of Australia's most popular bushranging songs, is probably a disguised version of 'Bold Jack Donahoe', one of many songs about an Irish convict turned bushranger that were banned by the authorities. The night before the battle of Glenrowan, the Kellys are said to have sung this song in Jones's Hotel, a grim omen of the fate that still awaited them.

While the police response to bushrangers was understandably predictable, the people's response was not. Many supported the Kellys and Ben Hall for example, but the response of 'Featherstonhaugh' or the narrator of Gordon's 'Wolf and Hound' was not atypical. Sometimes bushrangers were betrayed by their lovers or even their families, but perhaps the most imaginative response was that of Mrs Monroe of Monroe Station in Victoria. A bushranger bailed her up while she was cooking with hot fat. She promptly threw the fat in his face, tied him up, and sent for the police!

Featherstonhaugh

Barcroft Boake

Brookong station lay half-asleep
Dozed in the waning western glare
('Twas before the run had stocked with sheep
And only cattle depastured there)
As the Bluecap mob reined up at the door
And loudly saluted Featherstonhaugh.

'My saintly preacher,' the leader cried,
'I stand no nonsense, as you're aware,
I've a word for you if you'll step outside,
Just drop that pistol and have a care;
I'll trouble you, too, for the key of the store,
For we're short of tucker, friend Featherstonhaugh.'

The muscular Christian showed no fear,
Though he handed the key with but small delay;
He never answered the ruffian's jeer
Except by a look which seemed to say —
'Beware, my friend, and think twice before
you raise the devil in Featherstonhaugh.'

Two hours after he reined his horse
Up in Urana, and straightway went
To the barracks — the trooper was gone, of course,
Blindly nosing a week-old scent
Away in the scrub around Mount Galore.
'Confound the fellow!' quoth Featherstonhaugh.

'Will any man of you come with me
And give this Bluecap a dressing-down?'
They all regarded him silently
As he turned his horse, with scornful frown.
'You're curs, the lot of you, to the core —
I'll go by myself,' said Featherstonhaugh.

The scrub was thick on Urangeline
As he followed the tracks that twisted through
The box and dogwood and scented pine
(One of their horses had cast a shoe).
Steeped from his youth in forest lore,
He could track like a nigger, could Featherstonhaugh.

He paused as he saw the thread of smoke
From the outlaw camp, and he marked the sound
Of a hobble-check, as it sharply broke
The silence that held the scrub-land bound.
There were their horses — two, three, four —
'It's a risk, but I'll chance it!' quoth Featherstonhaugh.

He loosened the first, and it walked away,

But his comrade's silence could not be bought,
For he raised his head with a sudden neigh,
And plainly showed that he'd not be caught.
As a bullet sang from a rifle-bore —
'It's time to be moving,' quoth Featherstonhaugh.

The brittle pine, as they broke away,
Crackled like ice in a winter's ponds,
The strokes fell fast on the cones that lay
Buried beneath the withered fronds
That softly carpet the sandy floor —
Swept two on the tracks of Featherstonhaugh.

They struck that path that the stock had made,
A dustily-red, well-beaten track,
The leader opened a fusillade
Whose target was Featherston's stooping back.
But his luck was out, not a bullet tore
As much as a shred from Featherstonhaugh.

Rattle 'em, rattle 'em fast on the pad,
Where the sloping shades fell dusk and dim;
The manager's heart beat high and glad
For he knew the creek was a mighty swim.
Already he heard a smothered roar —
'They're done like a dinner!' quoth Featherstonhaugh.

It was almost dark as they neared the dam;
He struck the crossing as true as a hair;
For the space of a second the pony swam,
Then shook himself in the chill night air.
In a pine-tree shade on the further shore,
With his pistol cocked, stood Featherstonhaugh.

A splash — an oath — and a rearing horse,
A thread snapped short in the fateful loom,
The tide, unaltered, swept on its course
Though a fellow creature had met his doom:
Pale and trembling, and struck with awe,
Bluecap stood opposite Featherstonhaugh.

While the creek rolled muddily in between
The eddies played with the drowned man's hat.
The stars peeped out in the summer sheen,
A night-bird chirruped across the flat —
Quoth Bluecap, 'I owe you a heavy score,
And I'll live to repay it, Featherstonhaugh.'

But he never did, for he ran his race
Before he had time to fulfil his oath.
I can't think how, but, in any case,
He was hung, or drowned, or maybe both.
But whichever it was, he came no more
To trouble the peace of Featherstonhaugh.

Wolf and Hound

Adam Lindsay Gordon

You'll take my tale with a little salt;
But it needs none, nevertheless!
I was foiled completely — fairly at fault —
Disheartened, too, I confess!

At the splitters' tent I had seen the track
Of horse-hoofs fresh on the sward;
And though Darby Lynch and Donovan Jack
(Who could swear through a ten-inch board)

Solemnly swore he had not been there,
I was just as sure they lied;
For to Darby all that is foul was fair,
And Jack for his life was tried.

We had run him for seven miles or more
As hard as our nags could split;
At the start they were all too weary and sore,
And his was quite fresh and fit.

Young Marsden's pony had had enough
On the plain where the chase was hot;
We breasted the swell of the Bitterns' bluff,
And Mark couldn't raise a trot.

When the sea like a splendid silver shield
To the south-west suddenly lay,
On the brow of the Beetle the chestnut reeled —
And I bid good-bye to McCrea.

And I was alone when the mare fell lame
With a pointed flint in her shoe,
On the Stony Flats: I had lot the game!
— And what was a man to do?

I turned away with a fixed intent
And headed for Hawthorndell:
I could neither eat in the splitters' tent
Nor drink at the splitters' well.

I know that they gloried in my mishap,
And I cursed them between my teeth:
— A blood-red sunset through Brayton's Gap
Flung a lurid fire on the heath.

Could I reach the Dell? I had little reck,
And with scarce a choice of my own
I threw the reins on Miladi's neck —
I had freed her foot from the stone.

That season most of the swamps were dry,
And after so hard a burst

In the sultry noon of so hot a sky
She was keen to appease her thirst —

Or by instinct urged, or impelled by Fate
(I care not to solve these things)
Certain it is that she took me straight
To the Warrigal water springs!

I can shut my eyes and recall the ground
As though it were yesterday:
With shelf of the low, grey rocks girt round,
The springs in their basin lay.

Woods to the east and wolds to the north
In the sundown sullenly bloomed:
Dead black on a curtain of crimson cloth
Large peaks to the westward loomed.

I led Miladi through weed and sedge,
She leisurely drank her fill:
There was something close to the water's edge —
And my heart, with one leap, stood still!

For a horse's shoe and a rider's boot
Had left clean prints on the clay:
Someone had watered his beast on foot —
'Twas he! — he had gone! — which way?

Then the mouth of the cavern faced me fair
As I turned and fronted the rocks:
So at last I had pressed the wolf to his lair!
I had run to his earth the fox!

I thought so! Perhaps he was resting? Perhaps
He was waiting, watching for me?
I examined all my revolver caps;
I hitched my mare to a tree.

I had sworn to have him, alive or dead!
And to give him a chance was loth:
He knew his life had been forfeited!
He had even heard of my oath!

In my stockinged soles to the shelf I crept —
I crawled safe into the cave:
All silent! — if he was there he slept —
Not there — all dark as the grave! . . .

Through the crack I could hear the leaden hiss!
See the livid face through the flame!
How strange it seems that a man should miss
When his life depends on his aim!

There couldn't have been a better light
For him, nor a worse for me:
We were cooped up — caged like beasts for a fight —

And dumb as dumb beasts were we!

Flash! flash! — Bang! bang! — and we blazed away,
And the grey roof reddened and rang!
Flash! flash! — and I felt his bullet flay
The tip of my ear — Flash! bang!

Bang! flash! — and my pistol arm fell broke:
I struck with my left hand then:
— Struck at a corpse through a cloud of smoke!
I had shot him dead in his den.

The Ballad of Ben Hall's Gang

Come all you wild colonials
And listen to my tale;
A story of bushrangers' deeds
I will to you unveil.
'Tis of those gallant heroes,
Game fighters one and all;
And we'll sit and sing, Long live the King,
Dunn, Gilbert, and Ben Hall.

Ben Hall he was a squatter bloke
Who owned a thousand head;
A peaceful man he was until
Arrested by Sir Fred.
His home burned down, his wife cleared out,
His cattle perished all:
'They'll not take me a second time,'
Says valiant Ben Hall.

John Gilbert was a flash cove,
And John O'Meally too;
With Ben and Burke and Johnny Vane
They all were comrades true.
They rode into Canowindra
And gave a public ball.
'Roll up, roll up, and have a spree,'
Says Gilbert and Ben Hall.

They took possession of the town,
Including the public-houses,
And treated all the cockatoos
And shouted for their spouses.
They danced with all the pretty girls
And held a carnival.
'We don't hurt them who don't hurt us,'
Says Gilbert and Ben Hall.

They made a raid on Bathurst,
The pace was getting hot;
Buy Johnny Vane surrendered
After Micky Burke was shot,
O'Meally at Goimbla
Did like a hero fall;
'The game is getting lively,'
Says John Gilbert and Ben Hall.

Then Gilbert took a holiday,
Ben Hall got new recruits;
The Old Man and Dunleavy
Shared in the plunder's fruits.
Dunleavy he surrendered
And they jugged the Old Man tall —
So Johnny Gilbert came again
To help his mate, Ben Hall.

John Dunn he was a jockey bloke,
A-riding all the winners,
Until he joined Hall's gang to rob
The publicans and sinners;
And many a time the Royal Mail
Bailed up at John Dunn's call.
A thousand pounds is on their heads —
Dunn, Gilbert, and Ben Hall.

'Next week we'll visit Goulburn
And clean the banks out there;
So if you see the troopers,
Just tell them to beware;
Some day to Sydney city
We mean to pay a call,
And we'll take the whole damn country,'
Says Dunn, Gilbert, and Ben Hall.

Taking His Chance

Henry Lawson

They stood by door of the Inn on the rise;
May Carney looked up in the bushranger's eyes:
'Oh! why did you come? — it was mad of you, Jack;
You know that the troopers are out on your track.'
A laugh and a shake of his obstinate head —
'I wanted a dance, and I'll chance it,' he said.

Some twenty-odd bushmen had come to the ball,
But Jack from his youth had been known to them all,
And bushmen are soft where a woman is fair,
So the love of May Carney protected him there.
Through all the short evening — it seems like romance —
She danced with a bushranger taking his chance.

'Twas midnight — the dancers stood suddenly still,
For hoof-beats were heard on the side of the hill!
Ben Duggan, the drover, along the hillside
Came riding as only a bushman can ride.
He sprang from his horse, to the dancers he sped —
'The troopers are down in the gully!' he said.

Quite close to the shanty the troopers were seen.
'Clear out and ride hard for the ranges, Jack Dean!
Be quick!' said May Carney — her hand on her heart —
'We'll bluff them awhile, and 'twill give you a start.'
He lingered a moment — to kiss her, of course —
Then ran to the trees where he'd hobbled his horse.

She ran to the gate, and the troopers were there —
The jingle of hobbles came faint on the air —
Then loudly she screamed: it was only to drown
The treacherous clatter of sliprails let down.
But troopers are sharp, and she saw at a glance
That someone was taking a desperate chance.

They chased, and they shouted, 'Surrender, Jack Dean!'
They called him three times in the name of the Queen.
Then came from the darkness the clicking of locks;
The crack of a rifle was heard on the rocks!
A shriek, and a shout, and a rush of pale men —
And there lay the bushranger, chancing it then.

The sergeant dismounted and knelt on the sod —
'Your bushranging's over — make peace, Jack, with God!'
The dying man laughed — not a word he replied,
But turned to the girl who knelt down by his side.
He gazed in her eyes as she lifted his head:
'Just kiss me — my girl — and — I'll chance it,' he said.

The Wild Colonial Boy

There was a Wild Colonial Boy, John Dowling was his name,
Of poor but honest parents he was born in Castlemaine.
He was his father's only son, his mother's pride and joy,
And dearly did his parents love this Wild Colonial Boy.

Come, all my hearties, we'll roam the mountainside,
Together we will plunder, together we will ride,
We'll scour along the valleys and we'll gallop o'er the plains,
And we'll scorn to live in slavery, bound down with iron chains.

He was scarcely sixteen years of age when he left his father's home,
And through Victoria's countryside as bushranger to roam.
They put him in the iron gang in the government employ,
But never an iron on earth could hold the Wild Colonial Boy.

In sixty-one this daring youth commenced his wild career,
His courage was undaunted, no danger did he fear,
He stuck up the Beechworth mail coach, and robbed Judge MacEvoy,
Who trembling cold gave up his gold to the Wild Colonial Boy.

One day as he was riding the mountainside along,
A-listening to the kookaburra's happy laughing song,
He spied three mounted troopers — Kelly, Davis, and Fitzroy —
With a warrant for the capture of the Wild Colonial Boy.

'Surrender now, John Dowling, you see we're three to one.
Surrender, in the Queen's name, for you're a plunderin' son.'
He drew a pistol from his belt, and spun it like a toy.
'I'll fight but never surrender,' cried the Wild Colonial Boy.

He fired at Trooper Kelly, and brought him to the ground;
And in return from Davis received his mortal wound.
All shattered through the jaws he lay, still firing at Fitzroy;
And that's the way they captured him — the Wild Colonial Boy.

Stringybark Creek

A sergeant and three constables set out from Mansfield town
Near the end of last October for to hunt the Kellys down;
They started for the Wombat Hills and thought it quite a lark
When they camped upon the borders of a creek called Stringybark.

They had grub and ammunition there to last them many a week,
And next morning two of them rode out, all to explore the creek,
Leaving McIntyre behind them at the camp to cook the grub
And Lonergan to sweep the floor and boss the washing tub.

It was shortly after breakfast Mac thought he heard a noise
So gun in hand he sallied out to try and find the cause,
But he never saw the Kellys planted safe behind a log
So he sauntered back to smoke and yarn and wire into the prog.

But Ned Kelly and his comrades thought they'd like a nearer look,
For being short of grub they wished to interview the cook;
And of firearms and cartridges they found they had too few,
So they longed to grab the pistols and ammunition too.

Both the troopers at a stump alone they were well pleased to see
Watching as their billies boiled to made their pints of tea;
There they joked and chatted gaily never thinking of alarms
Till they heard the fearful cry behind, 'Bail up, throw up your arms!'

The traps they started wildly, and Mac then firmly stood
While Lonergan made tracks to try and gain the wood,
Reaching round for his revolver, but before he touched the stock
Ned Kelly pulled the trigger, fired, and dropped him like a rock.

Then after searching McIntyre all through the camp they went
And cleared the guns and cartridges and pistols from the tent,
But Kelly muttered sadly as he loaded up his gun,
'Oh what a — pity that the — tried to run.'

'Twas later in the afternoon the sergeant and his mate
Came riding blithely through the bush to meet a cruel fate.
'The Kelly's have the drop on you!' cried McIntyre aloud,
But the troopers took it as a joke and sat their horses proud.

Then trooper Scanlan made a move his rifle to unsling,
But to his heart a bullet sped and death was in the sting;
Then Kennedy leapt from his mount and ran for cover near,
And fought, a game man to the last, for all that life held dear.

The sergeant's horse ran from the camp alike from friend and foe,
And McIntyre, his life at stake, sprang to the saddle-bow
And galloped far into the night, a haunted, harassed soul,
Then like a hunted bandicoot hid in a wombat hole.

At dawn of day he hastened forth and made for Mansfield town
To break the news that made men vow to shoot the bandits down,
So from that hour the Kelly gang was hunted far and wide,
Like outlawed dingoes of the wild until the day they died.

Frank Gardiner

Oh Frank Gardiner is caught at last and lies in Sydney jail,
For wounding Sergeant Middleton and robbing the Mudgee mail.
For plundering of the gold escort, the Carcoar mail also;
And it was for gold he made so bold, and not so long ago.

His daring deeds surprised them all throughout the Sydney land,
And on his friends he gave a call, and quickly raised a band.
And fortune always favoured him, until this time of late,
Until Ben Hall and Gilbert met with their dreadful fate.

Young Vane, he has surrendered, Ben Hall's got his death wound,
And as for Johnny Gilbert, near Binalong was found,
He was all alone and lost his horse, three troopers came in sight,
And fought the three most manfully, got slaughtered in the fight.

Farewell, adieu, to outlawed Frank, he was the poor man's friend.
The Government has secured him, the laws he did offend.
He boldly stood his trial and answered in a breath,
'And do what you will, you can but kill; I have no fear of death!'

Day after day they remanded him, escorted from the bar,
Fresh charges brought against him from neighbours near and far,
And now it is all over; the sentence they have passed,
All sought to find a verdict, and 'Guilty' 'twas at last.

When lives you take, a warning boys, a woman never trust:
She will turn round, I will be bound, Queen's evidence, the first.
He's doing two-and-thirty years; he's doomed to serve the Crown,
And well may he say, he cursed the day he met with Mrs Brown.

Seafarers and River-rovers

Seafarers and River-rovers

In the early days of the Australian colonies, almost everyone would have been familiar with ships, perhaps recalling the long sea voyage from Europe, or short trips from Melbourne, Sydney or Van Diemen's Land, or trips on the river boats. It was often easier and cheaper to ship goods and produce than to haul it overland, and paddle-steamers were a common sight on the great Murray-Darling river system. 'A Nautical Yarn', one of the rare survivors of the songs of the river-boat crews, was popular when ports like Echuca could support 60 hotels, and the wharfs were lined with paddle-steamers taking on wool and other produce from the long queues of bullock wagons.

Navigating rivers was particularly difficult because of the changes brought by flood, drought and shifting snags, and the rivers claimed their share of wrecks. But perhaps wrecks are more commonly associated with seafaring, and the southern and eastern coasts of Australia certainly claimed many lives. Lawson's 'Wreck of the *Derry Castle*' evokes some of the horror of death at sea, and Gordon's 'From the Wreck' some of the desperation that people on shore faced by the wreck of a ship and the danger to the people on board. Perhaps it's not surprising that a poet who chose to die beside the sea should have written of it so often and so well: Gordon's 'The Swimmer' inspired one of Elgar's 'Sea Pictures', and his 'Exile's Farewell' provides us with a rare poem from on board a sailing ship setting out to sea. No doubt wrecks are more dramatic and romantic, but seafarers must have been glad of a poem where a ship actually stayed afloat!

The Wreck of the Derry Castle

Henry Lawson

Day of ending for beginnings!
Ocean hath another innings,
Ocean hath another score;
And the surges sing his winnings,
And the surges shout his winnings,
And the surges shriek his winnings,
All along the sullen shore.

Sing another dirge in wailing,
For another vessel sailing
With the shadow-ships at sea;
Shadow ships for ever sinking —
Shadow-ships whose pumps are clinking,
And whose thirsty holds are drinking
Pledges to Eternity.

Pray for souls of ghastly, sodden
Corpses, floating round untrodden
Cliffs, where nought but sea-drift strays:
Souls of dead men, in whose faces
Of humanity no trace is —
Not a mark to show their races —
Floating round for days and days.

* * *

Ocean's salty tongues are licking
Round the faces of the drowned,
And a cruel blade seems sticking
Through my heart, and turning round.
Heaven! shall *his* ghastly, sodden
Corpse float round for days and days?
Shall it dash 'neath cliffs untrodden,
Rocks where nought but sea-drift strays?

God in heaven! hide the floating,
Falling, rising, face from me;
God in heaven; stay the gloating,
Mocking singing of the sea!

The Swimmer

Adam Lindsay Gordon

With short, sharp, violent lights made vivid,
To southward far as the sight can roam,
Only the swirl of the surges livid,
The seas that climb and the surfs that comb.
Only the crag and the cliff to nor'ward,
And the rocks receding, and reefs flung forward,
And waifs wreck'd seaward and wasted shoreward
On shallows sheeted with flaming foam.

A grim, grey coast and a seaboard ghastly,
And shores trod seldom by feet of men —
Where the batter'd hull and the broken mast lie,
They have lain embedded these long years ten.
Love! when we wander'd here together,
Hand in hand through the sparkling weather,
From the heights and hollows of fern and heather,
God surely loved us a little then.

The skies were fairer and shores were firmer —
The blue sea over the bright sand roll'd;
Babble and prattle, and ripple and murmur,
Sheen of silver and glamour of gold —
And the sunset bath'd in the gulf to lend her
A garland of pinks and of purples tender,
A tinge of the sun-god's rosy splendour,
A tithe of his glories manifold.

Man's works are graven, cunning, and skilful
On earth, where his tabernacles are;
But the sea is wanton, the sea is wilful,
And who shall mend her and who shall mar?
Shall we carve success or record disaster
On the bosom of her heaving alabaster?
Will her purple pulse beat fainter or faster
For fallen sparrow or fallen star?

I would that with sleepy, soft embraces
The sea would fold me — would find me rest
In luminous shades of her secret places,
In depths where her marvels are manifest;
So the earth beneath her should not discover
My hidden couch — nor the heaven above her —
As a strong love shielding a weary lover,
I would have her shield me with shining breast.

When light in the realms of space lay hidden,
When life was yet in the womb of time,
Ere flesh was fettered to fruits forbidden,
And souls were wedded to care and crime,

Was the course foreshaped for the future spirit —
A burden of folly, a void of merit —
That would fain the wisdom of stars inherit,
And cannot fathom the seas sublime?

Under the sea or the soil (what matter?
The sea and the soil are under the sun),
As in the former days in the latter,
The sleeping or waking is known of none,
Surely the sleeper shall not awaken
To griefs forgotten or joys forsaken,
For the price of all things given and taken,
The sum of all things done and undone.

Shall we count offences or coin excuses,
Or weigh with scales the soul of a man,
Whom a strong hand binds and a sure hand looses,
Whose light is a spark and his life a span?
The seed he sow'd or the soil he cumber'd,
The time he served or the space he slumber'd,
Will it profit a man when his days are number'd,
Or his deeds since the days of his life began?

One, glad because of the light, saith, 'Shall not
The righteous Judge of all the earth do right,
For behold the sparrows on the house-tops fall not
Save as seemeth to Him good in His sight?'
And this man's joy shall have no abiding,
Through lights departing and lives dividing,
He is soon as one in the darkness hiding,
One loving darkness rather than light.

A little season of love and laughter,
Of light and life, and pleasure and pain,
And a horror of outer darkness after,
And dust returneth to dust again.
Then the lesser life shall be as the greater,
And the lover of life shall join the hater,
And the one thing cometh sooner or later,
And no one knoweth the loss or gain.

Love of my life! we had lights in season —
Hard to part from, harder to keep —
We had strength to labour and souls to reason,
And seed to scatter and fruits to reap.
Though time estranges and fate disperses,
We have *had* our loves and our loving-mercies;
Though the gifts of the light in the end are curses,
Yet bides the gift of the darkness — sleep!

See! girt with tempest and wing'd with thunder,
And clad with lightning and shod with sleet,
The strong winds treading the swift waves sunder

The flying rollers with frothy feet.
One gleam like a bloodshot sword-blade swims on
The sky-line, staining the green gulf crimson,
A death stroke fiercely dealt by a dim sun,
That strikes through his stormy winding sheet.

Oh! brave white horses! you gather and gallop,
The storm sprite loosens the gusty reins;
Now the stoutest ship were the frailest shallop,
In your hollow backs, or your high arch'd manes.
I would ride as never a man has ridden,
In your sleepy, swirling surges hidden,
To gulfs foreshadow'd through straits forbidden,
Where no light wearies and no love wanes.

A Nautical Yarn

I sing of a capting not unknown to fame;
A naval commander, Bill Jinks was his name,
Who sailed where the Murray's clear waters do flow,
Did this freshwater shellback, with his Yeo heave a yeo.

To the Port of Wahgunyah his wessel was bound
When night comes upon him and darkness around;
Not a star on the waters its clear light did throw;
But the wessel sped onward with a Yeo heave a yeo.

'Oh , capting, oh! capting, let's make for the shore,
For the winds they do rage and the winds they do roar!'
'Nay, nay,' said the capting, 'though the fierce winds may blow
I will stick to my wessel with a Yeo heave a yeo.'

'Oh, capting, oh! capting, the waves sweep the deck,
Oh, capting, oh! capting, we'll soon be a wreck —
To the river's deep bosom each seaman will go!'
But the capting laughed lightly, with his Yeo heave a yeo.

'Farewell to the maiding — the girl I adore;
Farewell to my friends — I shall see them no more!'
The crew shrieked in terror, the capting he swore —
They had stuck on a sandbank, so the men walked ashore.

The Song of the Surf
Adam Lindsay Gordon

White steeds of ocean, that leap with a hollow and wearisome roar
On the bar of ironstone steep, not a fathom's length from the shore,
Is there never a seer nor sophist can interpret your wild refrain,
When speech the harshest and roughest is seldom studied in vain?
My ears are constantly smitten by that dreary monotone,
In a hieroglyphic 'tis written — 'tis spoken in a tongue unknown;
Gathering, growing, and swelling, and surging, and shivering, say!
What is the tale you are telling? what is the drift of your lay?

You come, and your crests are hoary with the foam of your countless
    years;
You break, with a rainbow of glory, through the spray of your
    glittering tears.
Is your song a song of gladness? a paean of joyous might?
Or a wail of discordant sadness for the wrongs you never can right?
For the empty seat by the ingle? for children reft of their sire?
For the bride, sitting sad, and single, and pale, by the flickering fire?
For your ravenous pools of suction? for your shattering billow swell?
For your ceaseless work of destruction? for your hunger insatiable?

Not far from this very place, on the sand and the shingle dry,
He lay, with his batter'd face upturned to the frowning sky.
When your waters wash'd and swill'd high over his drowning head,
When his nostrils and lungs were filled, when his feet and hands
    were as lead,
When against the rock he was hurl'd and suck'd again to the sea,
On the shores of another world, on the brink of eternity,
On the verge of annihilation, did it come to that swimmer strong,
The sudden interpretation of your mystical weird-like song?

'Mortal! that which thou askest, ask not thou of the waves;
Fool! thou foolishly taskest us — we are only slaves;
Might more mighty, impels us — we must our lot fulfil,
He who gathers and swells us curbs us, too, at His will.
Think'st thou the wave that shatters questioneth His decree?
Little to us it matters, and naught it matters to thee.
Not thus, murmuring idly, we from our duty would swerve,
Over the world spread widely ever we labour and serve.'

An Exile's Farewell
Adam Lindsay Gordon

The ocean heaves around us still
With long and measured swell,
The autumn gales our canvas fill,
Our ship rides smooth and well.
The broad Atlantic's bed of foam
Still breaks against our prow;
I shed no tears at quitting home,
Nor will I shed them now!

Against the bulwarks on the poop
I lean, and watch the sun
Behind the red horizon stoop —
His race is nearly run.
Those waves will never quench his light,
O'er which they seem to close,
To-morrow he will rise as bright
As he this morning rose.

How brightly gleams the orb of day
Across the trackless sea!
How lightly dance the waves that play
Like dolphins in our lee!
The restless waters seem to say,
In smothered tones to me,
How many thousand miles away
My native land must be!

Speak, Ocean! is my Home the same,
Now all is new to me? —
The tropic sky's resplendent flame,
The vast expanse of sea?
Does all around her, yet unchanged,
The well-known aspect wear?
Oh! can the leagues that I have ranged
Have made no difference there?

How vivid Recollection's hand
Recalls the scene once more!
I see the same tall poplars stand
Beside the garden door;
I see the bird-cage hanging still;
And where my sister set
The flowers in the window-sill —
Can they be living yet?

Let woman's nature cherish grief,
I rarely heave a sigh
Before emotion takes relief
In listless apathy;

While from my pipe the vapours curl
Towards the evening sky,
And 'neath my feet the billows whirl
In dull monotony!

The sky still wears the crimson streak
Of Sol's departing ray,
Some briny drops are on my cheek,
'Tis but the salt sea spray!
Then let our barque the ocean roam,
Our keel the billows plough;
I shed no tears at quitting home,
Nor will I shed them now!

The Light on the Wreck

Henry Lawson

Out there by the rocks, at the end of the bank,
In the mouth of the river the *Wanderer* sank.
She is resting between the blue water and green,
And only her masts and her funnel are seen;
And you see, as day fades to its last crimson fleck,
On her foremost a lantern — a light on a wreck.

'Tis a light on a wreck, warning ships to beware
Of the drowned iron hull of the *Wanderer* there;
And the ships that come in and go out in the night
Keep a careful look out for the *Wanderer's* light.
There are rules for the harbour and rules for the wave;
But all captains stand clear of a ship in her grave.

And the stories of strong lives that ended in wrecks
Might be likened to lights over derelict decks;
Like the light where, in sight of the streets of the town,
In the mouth of the channel the *Wanderer* went down;
Keep a watch from the desk, as they watch from the deck;
Keep a watch from your home for the light on the wreck.

But the lights on the wrecks since creation began
Have been shining in vain for the vagabond clan.
They will never take warning, they will not beware;
They have for their watch words, 'What matter?' 'What care?'
They steer without compass, and sail without check,
Till they drift to their grave 'neath a light on a wreck.

Index of Titles